FC 107

D0189356

Doris Tijerino
Inside the
Nicaraguan Revolution

DORIS TIJERINO
Inside the
Nicaraguan
Revolution

As Told to Margaret Randall

Translated from the Spanish by Elinor Randall

New Star Books • Vancouver

New Star Books Ltd.
2504 York Avenue
Vancouver, B.C. V6K 1E3
Canada

Canadian Cataloguing in Publication Data

Randall, Margaret, 1938-
    Doris Tijerino

    Translation of "somos millones . . ." :
    la vida de Doris Maria
    ISBN 0-919888-84-4
    ISBN 0-919888-83-6 pa.

    1. Tijerino, Doris. 2. Nicaragua — Politics
and government — 1937 3. Revolutionists —
Nicaragua. I. Tijerino, Doris.
F1527.R3513   972.85'04   C78-002113-4

ACKNOWLEDGMENTS

All the graphic material for this book has been taken from the Nicaraguan newspapers *La Prensa* and *Novedades* (1961-1975), the magazine *VANGUARDIA* (publication of Nicaraguan exiles in Los Angeles, California, the United States), the news agency *Prensa Latina* and the magazine *Bohemia* (both of Havana, Cuba).

Photocopy work by Luis Marrero, Mayra A. Martinez and Rogelio Arias.

For the great amount of valued help received, I want to especially thank the Sandinist Front for National Liberation of Nicaragua; and comrades Robert Cohen, Pat and David Gallagher, Dino Garcia Carrera, Francisco Garzon Cespedes, Stasia Madrigal, Juan Luis Martin and Margarita Zimmerman. *M.R.*

Publisher's Note:
The publisher wishes to thank Daphne Morrison for her contribution to the production of this book. We'd also like to thank Carmen Rodriguez, Bill Deacon and Rod Haynes for their assistance.

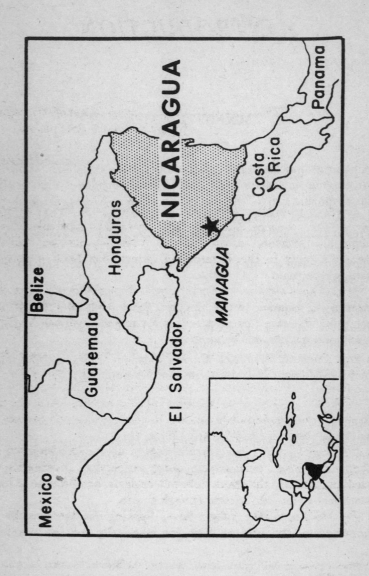

INTRODUCTION

"There are millions of us, Doris Maria of Nicaragua,
a fighting woman of the people . . . "

Ricardo Morales*

Doris Tijerino and I want people everywhere to know the truth about the present situation in Nicaragua, particularly the repressive measures of the dictator, Anastasio Somoza, and the people's reply to the dictatorship, which has been a lengthy struggle for national liberation.

In this book we present that struggle through the life story of a woman—a woman whose life has been shaped through the struggle. Because this woman is a Nicaraguan, we can begin to know and understand Nicaragua.

Nicaraguan women are waking up. Like women in dependent countries everywhere they have been doubly exploited, by capitalism and imperialism, and also simply because they are women. They are coming to realise that the choices which life has to offer under imperialism and the dictatorship are no choices at all. Today they are beginning to reject them.

For working class and peasant women the choices imposed on them have been: semi-slavery domestic service, prostitution or stealing, death in the street from tuberculosis, or a lifetime of hard work just to be able to earn enough to eat.

For women of the ruling class, fighting for the crumbs of imperialism, the choices keep you physically fed but mentally

* From a poem entitled "Doris Maria, comrade" by Ricardo Morales, La Aviacion Prison, 1970.

starved: the "success" of a New York model, working for charity as a social butterfly, becoming the lover of a security agent . . .

But Nicaraguan women are waking up: as a people, collectively, and in growing numbers. As the revolutionary, Ricardo Morales, wrote to his comrade, a militant woman who is the central figure of this book, " . . . there are millions of us, Doris Maria of Nicaragua . . ." Among those millions we now count millions of women.

In Nicaragua the tyranny of one family, the Somozas, has a continuous history of over forty years. That family has sold Nicaragua to imperialism and is now protected by it.

Peasants are raped and killed every day. Political prisoners are tortured in the president's own house—sometimes by the president himself. That is if they are not immediately killed. We know of one case where a peasant was taken prisoner only because he happened to have a photograph of General Sandino.

Augusto Cesar Sandino was a leader in the fight against US imperialism and military operations in Nicaragua in the thirties. The "Sandinist" struggle, as it is called, is a basic part of the tradition of the Nicaraguan people—a tradition that forty years of military dictatorship has been unable to stamp out.

In the international division of labour under the capitalist system, Nicaragua has been assigned the role of supplying cheap labour and raw materials for the production of cotton, meat, coffee, and sugar. (These products make up 60 per cent of the country's exports.) The vast profits of the big cotton, coffee, sugar, and banana companies are based exclusively on the superexploitation of the agricultural workers, an exploitation which hits working women with special intensity.

Somoza's military dictatorship carries out its repressive role in order to secure foreign investments. It hands over enormous concessions of land for the exploration of non-renewable resources such as oil and minerals. It supplies the capitalist market with agribusiness products and at the same time operates hand in glove with the North American mafia and Cuban expatriates, who promote investments in "tourism," such as drugs, night clubs, gambling and so on.

Here's what this system of domination produces:

According to the 1971 census, out of the country's entire

economically active population of 504,240 persons, 79 per cent are men and 21 per cent are women. (According to the same source the country's population is about two million.)

The International Organization of Labour in the United Nations reports that Nicaragua had 22,000 servants in 1969, and only 10,000 teachers that same year.

Illiteracy stands at 70 per cent. In the rural areas it is over 86 per cent, and, as in other countries, this figure is higher among women. Among peasants in the department of Matagalpa, where Doris comes from, it reaches 93.2 per cent. Between 1954 and 1959 only 9.3 per cent of the students reached high school, and scarcely 0.6 per cent university.

Before the 1972 earthquake—which left 250,000 homeless and between 20,000 and 30,000 dead—statistics show that there were 6.2 persons to a house. Only 16.1 per cent of the population had potable water, 8 per cent had sewage service, and only 9 per cent had inside plumbing.

Infant mortality comes to 102 per 1,000 live births, one of the highest ratios in Latin America. Fifty per cent of the deaths take place among those under the age of 14. The deaths are from malnutrition, gastroenteritis, tuberculosis, and other illnesses caused by these kinds of living conditions.

The ideology of imperialism and capitalism is transmitted by the education system, through text books and study programs which have the full blessing of the Nicaraguan government.

All the facts which we have mentioned—in addition to the countless ones we have no room for here—point to a system of blatant and violent exploitation in Nicaragua. The system is maintained through a planned and coordinated counter-revolutionary strategy, which is a key characteristic of imperialism and which is in effect throughout Central America. It was put into practice first in Nicaragua back in 1967 as an answer to the revolutionary struggle which, headed by the Sandinist Front for National Liberation (FSLN), began in 1958, and continues today.

The institution in charge of counter-insurgency and repression is the CONDECA (Council of Central American Defense), a structure of intermediate military command between the Central American armies and the US Department of Defense. The strategy consists of ensuring North American investors that Nicaragua is a "safe" place in which to invest. This is done by a combined system of military repression of the people and programs of "Civic Action." (Nicaragua is the Latin American country with the greatest number of soldiers, officers, and police trained directly by the United States.) These programs of the National Guard, Peace Corps and other agencies of imperialism consist for instance of vast birth control plans which include the sterilization of children and adults. Although Nicaragua is one of the least populated countries in the world (14 inhabitants per square kilometer), one third of its people have been forced into exile by economic oppression and repression. It is absurd to argue the need to control the population growth. The only motivation of birth control programs like these is a desire to crush the working and peasant classes—the potential revolutionaries.

Despite the daily violence, the Nicaraguan people have always struggled against it. Women have been active in this struggle since the popular Sandinist war of liberation. Three outstanding and heroic fighters in these times were Maria de Altamirano, Concha Alday, and Blanca Arauz. In the last twenty years working women like young Luisa Amanda Espinosa (killed in combat), peasant women like Maria Castil (raped and murdered), and an ever increasing number of students have fought together with the people against the military dictatorship of Somoza.

This Central American country, Nicaragua, has been desecrated and outraged, but it has a future which is being built by the struggle of many men and women like Doris.

Doris' story is not ended. It is a living story that continues. It belongs to one woman but it is not unique. It is repeated. It is multiplied. It is growing.

Margaret Randall
Havana, 1976

ü

On Thursday, April 13, 1978, eight kilometers from the Honduras border in a village called Los Encinos—in the Tablon Valley—a battle took place between the Sandinist forces and the Nicaraguan National Guard. According to information released by the National Guard itself, one Sandinist combatant—Mauricio Cajina Perez—was killed, another managed to escaped, and Doris Maria Tijerino Haslam was taken prisoner.

Inside and outside Nicaragua, the liberation forces immediately made public this situation, hoping to raise international opinion around the fact that Doris is—once more—being held by the dictatorship. No amount of support is too much for prisoners in the hands of criminals like Somoza. The Nicaraguan National Guard has frequently tortured prisoners to death and written it off as "death in battle," forced prisoners to try to run for it and applied the well-known *ley de fuga* (shoot-to-kill escape law) or simply made men and women disappear under a blanket of silence.

The reader of this book, which was written during 1974-75, will find other events since updated by history. Life in Nicaragua today moves at a speed equivalent to the people's all-out need for freedom.

Rene Tejada, who tells the story of his brother's death by torture in this book, was himself killed in a battle at the beginning of 1975. On November 8 and 9 of the following year, important FSLN leaders Eduardo Contreras and Carlos Fonseca Amador fell in different parts of the country. A listing of other losses could be made and it would never be up to date at the time of a given publication deadline.

In a so-far unexplained action (signs point to CIA or other mafia-type interference) the bourgeois opposition leader Pedro Joaquin Chamorro was gunned down in late 1977.

More important would be a listing of the people's battles, the increasing popular support and organization behind the vanguard Sandinist National Liberation Front, as well as other groups convinced that only through sound political struggle coordinated with all-out people's war will the dynasty tumble.

Between October 12 and 19, 1977, the FSLN launched a nation-wide offensive which is still going strong. Important sectors

of the working class, whole villages in the countryside, Indian
tribes in their entirety and a vigorous student movement are
proving to be the vanguard in a clear-cut struggle to victory. There
are cities like Masaya, which can only be described as heroic:
there's no other word to do justice to masses of people, armed with
little more than homemade weapons, maintaining an all-out
defense against the repressive forces for days at a time.

Somoza is losing his grip daily, and opposition to his criminal
and crazed regime increases even among the bourgeois
opposition. At this writing—April 1978—the US is still backing
the monster, and that's what's keeping him in power. The
Pentagon continues to coordinate the Central American Defense
Organization (CONDECA) but operations like *"Aguila Z"* at the end
of 1976—in which 3000 Salvadorian and Guatemalan soldiers
joined US Rangers and Nicaraguan National Guard in combing the
Jalapa and other mountain areas—have been unable to route out or
even considerably damage guerrilla units. The presence of
"advisors"—and now even troops—from the United States, Brazil
and the old Saigonese Puppet Army, is repeatedly denounced by
the Nicaraguan people.

Doris, this book remains a battle cry from all our sisters. It pays
homage, as well, to Arlen Siu, Claudia Chamorro, Maria
Castilblanco, Julia Herrera and Mildred Abuanza—fallen in
combat since this book was written; Charlotte Baltodano Egner,
whose eloquent prison testimony reveals further details of
Somoza's dungeons; Liana Benavides, Ruth Marcenaro, Rosa
Argentina Ortiz and Maria Martha Beltran who turned their trial
into a cry for justice heard around the world; the housewives who
bang their pots and pans in a coordinated nationwide effort to call
attention to their country's lot; and the untold numbers of
anonymous women who have joined the struggle, died in it, or
continue to fight.

M.R.
Havana, April 1978

1943 - 1955

"I wasn't tall or blond, nor did I have blue eyes; I was a Nicaraguan . . ."

I was born in 1943 in Matagalpa, a city in the north of the country, in the north-central part. It is a city in the mountainous region where the main economic activity is agriculture, the cultivation of coffee and cattle raising.

The city of Matagalpa is a town pretending to be a city. It is head of the department and therefore has had the rank of city for a hundred and some odd years. Its streets were paved only recently. Motorized vehicles have been there for only a few years. I remember that my older brother, scarcely eighteen, rode from the farm to college on horseback. Matagalpa's houses usually have one storey, and they're made of cement and *taquezal*—earth, like adobe.

Its commercial activity is limited; there are few large commercial establishments; up to a few years ago there were only a small number of them, where they sold work clothes, and a lot of little businesses dealing in grain, a few banks and coffee-buying houses. Matagalpa is a small city where everybody knows each other. There's quite a familiar atmosphere. Matagalpa's high society is a very closed society and one of the most reactionary. Very Catholic, conservative and traditional.

There are many foreigners in Matagalpa. The land belongs to foreigners, mainly the English and Germans. They came a long time ago, practically when colonization of the virgin lands began and especially when the cultivation of coffee was introduced in the 1850s onward, up to 1870.

Most of these families have been absorbed by the center, although some are making efforts to preserve their traditions; a

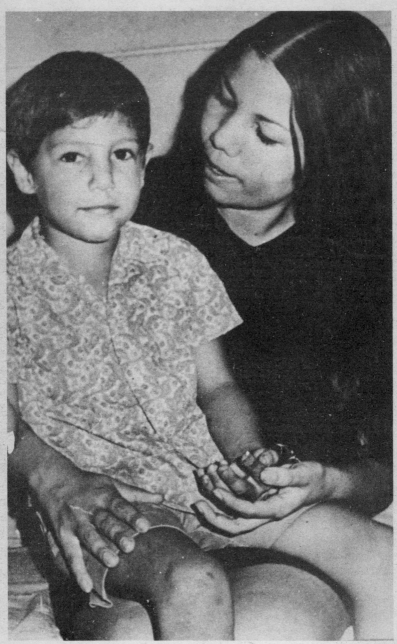

Doris Tijerino and her son, May 1971.

Doris Tijerino in one of Somoza's prisons.

thing that makes them appear ridiculous in some cases . . . For example, they have a cemetery for foreigners, located opposite the cemetery for native Nicaraguans. When the women of these families marry nationals, they lose the right to be buried in "their" cemetery; this is almost a dishonour. Yet the Nicaraguan woman who marries one of these "foreigners" acquires the right to be buried there.

Up to a few years ago there was a club for foreigners. The pillar of this club was the Calley-Dagnall family, an example of the foreign-colonizing oligarchy which exploits the region. This family constituted a commercial association dedicated to the purchase of coffee for export. Besides, it acted in the capacity of a money lender which, with a drop in the price of coffee, allowed it to acquire a lot of property.

When these people broadened their economic activity, always at the cost of the sweat and blood of the local population, they moved their main business firm to Managua. Today it is one of the principal houses for the purchase of coffee. With these people's move to Managua, the club for foreigners practically disappeared. This was during the early 1950s. Through this club they tried to impress on people the difference between foreigners and nationals, and to teach their children, who were Nicaraguans, to feel that difference. In other words, they taught them to discriminate.

I remember that in this club they gave parties for children in accordance with English customs—for example, they celebrated Christmas with a pine tree, without the nativity scene . . . They also organized a "tea" one day a week for children and another for adults. They accustomed them to classes given in English . . .

As a child I took part in some of this club's activities—and I really learned to differentiate, only in a sense contrary to the one they tried to teach me. I felt really different; I wasn't tall or blond, nor did I have blue eyes; I was a Nicaraguan. It was in these early days that I had the first notions of what discrimination meant.

"A book by Gorky, which was later to have great importance in my own life . . ."

My mother was the daughter of English parents. Number fourteen, the last. She was left without parents when very young. My grandfather died when she was about seven and my grandmother died shortly afterward. Then, the youngest children were distributed among older ones who were already married. It was my mother's lot to live a very hard childhood. She was an orphan and separated from her brothers and sisters in times when there was great repression in the countryside combined with bad economic conditions. There was an enormous quantity of land that couldn't be profitable because there was a world crisis and coffee was worth nothing, therefore the land wasn't worth anything.

She was a very restless person and liked to read; she never could study because she wasn't used to it. It wasn't elegant for girls to learn any more than to read and write, and afterward they were sent to a school of some French nuns where they learned feminine culture which included embroidery, weaving, cooking and housekeeping. Still very young, being eighteen, my mother married my father. Earlier, she had married another man from whom she was separated.

Before starting school I spent a good part of my childhood in the countryside, on my grandparents' farm. When I talk about my grandparents I'm really talking about my mother's sister and her husband—that sister raised my mother when her parents died. We always called them grandparents.

We enjoyed a lot of freedom on the farm; they allowed us to go everywhere freely. We used to go to the coffee plantations and we became friendly with other peasant children, sons and daughters of the servants, and so on. There were a great many servants in the house, with their children, who had to be classified as "children of the house," or servants who were obliged to play with us and take care of us.

"Children of the house" are a kind of servant class. Girls and boys of very poor families are given to the landowners or middle class people to be "taught to work." They receive no salary at all . . .

There was a totally paternalistic relationship between my

grandparents and the servants. Some servants had been there for many years, came as children, married and had their children there. One of them died there after almost fifty years of working on the farm.

On our part the relationship with the peasants or with the "children of the house" was also established in paternalistic terms. Maybe not consciously, because we were very young to have that kind of relationship imposed on us, but the family environment and our social class gave it this character. The peasant himself was so used to it that without proposing it to us the servant-master relationship was always established, even in games. When we played games we were always the leaders.

My mama's family, after 1927, was in very bad economic straits due to the decrease in the price of coffee and because their capital depended on their lands which were situated in the northern zone where part of the war against the invasion of the Marines broke out. One of my mama's brothers died in this war, my uncle Charles Haslan; he was shot by a patrol of the Sandinist army.

My mama's brothers had stayed in the zone because they were not against Sandino. They were English, and the intervention was maintained by the *gringos* who were the principal rivals of the English in the country on the economic plane. The attitude of my mother's family was not against Sandino, but neither did they take part in the fight. Their nationality or origin placed them in a neutral position although their class interests were opposed to those of the Sandinist army. They remained on the sidelines.

Sandino let them remain there and they paid a tax like all the landowners who stayed in the zone. But apparently on one occasion one of my mama's brothers didn't pay the tax, and General Sandino had given the order that foreigners who refused to pay would be shot.

Afterward, and in books containing some records of the times, I realized that he'd been accused of being a traitor. I don't know if he committed some act of treason against General Sandino or if they called him a traitor because he refused to pay the tax. That's one of the reasons why my mama's family hasn't backed Sandino, although they've never been sympathetic to the Somozas or to the Guard either. They're conservatives by tradition.

My mama, on the other hand, had the chance to be associated

with people of the left, with revolutionaries. Part of her childhood and youth was spent in the midst of great poverty. She liked to read and she understood the Sandino struggle. At various times I remember that she explained to me that she understood the reasons General Sandino could have had for being inflexible with foreigners, with anyone who had opposed his struggle, and that there were many ways of opposition: not participating or refusing to pay the tax. She used to tell me it was an unfortunate thing that the man shot happened to be her brother, but so it had to be.

Later, when she had grown up, when she was sixteen or seventeen, she met some South Americans who were visiting the country. They had a magazine and were interested in writing articles on Nicaragua. I think one or two of them were members of the Chilean Communist Party.   And they apparently gave my mama one of Gorky's books that was later going to be very important in my own life . . .

But that was later . . .

"... stories of how the gringos *persecuted them . . ."*

My grandmother used to tell us stories of how the *gringos* persecuted them and how they had to sleep in the hills, and how sometimes at the same time they had to hide from guerrilla bands, for inasmuch as they were foreigners and in the country or in the zone, every foreigner was sometimes considered a "Yankee . . ." The stories were unbiased. She told us the facts. When we were given some focus, it was my mama who gave it. She was very emphatic about explaining to us that the Sandinists weren't bandits and that Sandinist was a term used by the Guard. She also told us about the *gringos'* cruelties with the peasants and Sandinists.

Once a patrol commanded by a Yankee officer came to a plantation which had been robbed a few days before by some unknown people. The plantation owners told a *gringo* about the robbery and he promised them to recover what was lost. After some days the patrol returned to the city and again stopped at the plantation. The Yankee officer told the owners that he had not been able to find what they had lost but that he had a surprise for them instead, and asked them to keep one of his mules. There was a saddle bag on the mule's back. In a few days there was an unbearable odor around the mule, so bad that it made the people of the house go outside to see what was happening. They told me it was a frightful spectacle for them when they opened the saddle bag and found the heads of two peasants in it, and a paper that said though he hadn't been able to recover the stolen articles, he was leaving the heads of the "supposed" robbers with them.

My mama had a peasant friend, a very old lady, who was twelve years old at the time of Sandino's struggle, and this peasant woman told us how they had to go away from their houses, from their places, because the Yankees were bombing entire mountains. She told us what it cost a peasant to move from one place to another, because they were arrested and killed as suspects by the *retenes** who were everywhere.

" . . . there had to be rich and poor . . . "

When I was very small I always saw the question from the angle of Christian charity. But it was a certain kind of charity. When a child would die on the farm, we'd take flowers, candles and the shroud we were going to wrap the child in. We'd go constantly, because children in the countryside die very frequently.

At that time the differences I settled on were between rich and poor. I didn't see beyond that and though I thought it unjust, I believed that's the way it was. That's what I was taught in the religious schools. That there had to be rich and poor, and that those who had money ought to be concerned with the well-being of those who didn't. In other words, I ruled my actions in accordance with that Christian doctrine.

Once—and this is one of the memories that has impressed me most—when I was seven or eight years old, a child with the last name of Diaz died in one of the little huts on the plantation, and they notified the ranch house. We were given the shroud and

---

* A *reten* is a control post established in moments of revolutionary activity for the purpose of detecting its participants.

candles to deliver. The shroud was ready quickly because it was one of the activities we devoted ourselves to—sewing shrouds for the children and keeping on hand a certain amount of clothing for the peasant children when they were going to be baptized or when they were born . . .

We went running because it was relatively nearby, and in great surprise we found that the child had gotten up—he was a child more or less our age—and he got up saying, "Mama, I want to shit." What he had was an enormous amount of parasites and the intestinal worms made him have an attack, the kind that happens very often in the countryside. And his parents thought he was dead. This affected me so much that I never even forgot the place that hut was in, or the people who were there at the time . . .

They later took that house away from the place, ordered it torn out. It was a little tiny shack, with mud walls and a dirt floor, like so many of them . . . It was miserable, with everything on one single floor. The family must have been very large, like all peasant families, and they must have lived with as little privacy as did all the peasant families around there. I remember that on the same floor—all there was of the house—was a cooking place, a cot (where the little "dead boy" lay) and a hammock. No latrine. They must have attended to their bodily needs in a ditch behind the hut . . .

I was afraid to go by there—always remembering that child. And I had to pass the place often because it was on the road I used to take to where they measured the coffee, one of my grandparents' principal sources of wealth.

There were many people on the plantation; it was a very large tract of land. I've never known exactly how large it was, but there was a valley with about two hundred people living in it, and there were other houses, with colonists, insecure peasants settled on the tracts. A large coffee and cattle ranch.

I went to a nuns' school when I was about six, and left in 1955. There's a lot to say about the shaping we received there, but the story would be endless. I believe there's one fact that can characterize the way girls are trained in that kind of school. We had a project we called "clothes for the poor," consisting in our collecting old clothes, shoes, and sometimes food, that we would later distribute among the poor. Each one or each group of two or

three girls had its "poor people," visited them and took them the
things collected. It was the best way of teaching us that "there had
to be rich and poor people in the world, and that the rich must help
the poor," without making us feel bad because of this situation,
since we were helping.

It's a good way to make us insensitive. In other words, we were
being shaped "to fulfill our mission in society." At present I don't
hear from my friends of those days very often; most of the time I
find out about them from the social columns of the newspaper, and
they really are playing their "role" of "ladies."

"Oh, the life of my mother: such contradictions . . ."

My mama, then, with a lot of patience and a lot of subtlety,
explained to me—she never stated things openly and counter to
the teachings I was receiving in school—but she explained to me
that some things were not so certain or so fair . . . She even
explained to me which of the peasants who were there had been
owners of those lands. Because of conditions of oppression and
economic exploitation that permitted such a system over the poor
peasants, they had seen themselves in need of handing over their
lands to the plantation.

I thought she wasn't going to church, that she wasn't
frequenting church, but it wasn't until I was twelve or thirteen that
she told me she wasn't a Catholic. That is to say, she didn't
practice religion. I imagine that she had been baptized and all that,
but she didn't go to church.

It was at that time when she handed over to me a series of books,
among them that book by Gorky she had kept from her own
youth, since she had met those South Americans I mentioned
earlier. It was Gorky's *The Mother*. She had kept it for me to read
when I was fifteen but she allowed me to read it earlier. That book
had great influence on me. And she brought other books for me
too—books like *Mamita Yunay* by Carlos Luis Falla . . . *Mamita
Yunay* is a book telling about the exploitation suffered by the
peasants and workers on the banana plantations. Falla is a Costa
Rican writer.

My mother always, constantly, made me see the relationship

between North American imperialism and the dictatorship of the Somozas, and the situation of the Nicaraguan people . . .

Oh, the life of my mother: such contradictions . . . As I told you, she had married very young, at about sixteen, before her marriage to my father. There were no children from that first marriage. They say "dirty rags are washed at home." The things they consider scandalous—"dirty rags"—like a marriage ending in divorce and then another marriage, all that stayed inside the house. In fact I didn't find out my mother had been married twice till a little while before she died.

She never complained about the marriage to my father, but I don't believe, given the kind of person she was, that she could have been very happy. My papa didn't have any political restlessness; he was the son of a good family, with a liberal militancy but with a totally reactionary mentality. He belongs to the bourgeoisie of Leon, in the eastern part of the country.

Later, now having children and everything, I know my mama was somewhat politically active even against my papa's will. Back in 1947, there were some massive protests going on in the country because of dishonesty in the elections . . . She told me about it.

I remember that around that time the Guard wanted to arrest my papa because he was an independent liberal, not a Somoza liberal—the Liberal Party was divided into independent and Somoza liberals. I've never forgotten the violent way the Guard arrived. They didn't find my papa, I remember they brought a truck filled with people; they were rounding them up like animals. At that moment it was night and my grandmother—my mother's sister who took charge of raising her when her mother died—got us up at midnight and told us we had to pray because the Guard was very bad and capable of killing all those people rounded up in that truck . . .

I was very small when all this happened. I was about five years old. I remember she got us up and made us kneel at the edge of our beds to pray that the Guard wouldn't do anything while on the road to the people they had in the truck.

"But it turned out that the land they were going to colonize belonged to the native community . . ."

For a long time I felt guilty that there were poor children, especially on the plantation. I felt somewhat obligated to find a solution to their situation, and I recall having stolen some small fruit to give them that was stored in the cellar.

A little old woman, a peasant, used to tell my grandmother that I wasn't going to come to a good end because I wasn't "prudent," that I questioned everything, that I looked people in the eyes and enjoyed giving away things from the plantation.

At Christmas time it was the custom to give toys to the children on the plantation. Very cheap presents were bought for everyone—sort of mass production. Our own Christmas was celebrated on the farm, in the presence of all those children, with all our gifts. I realized that we should never have celebrated Christmas in the presence of the other children who were only watching us. Any child with a minimum of sensitivity would have to feel affected by that situation. But my grandparents were in that respect a result of their class . . .

Also when I was very small—I must have been nine or ten—my family was in the habit of visiting another plantation nearby, within walking distance. It belonged to some Danes. The lady of the house had a lot of scars on her arm, and this impressed me. She was a little person and I was impressed by the number of welts that lady had on her arm.

I asked my family about it—the older members. I was told it was the result of an attack she had suffered from some Indians from the region. I was told that when these Danes arrived in about 1920, brought in by Diego Chamorro, this lady—who now must be a very old woman with grandchildren, and even great grandchildren—was a very young woman who had only one daughter and her husband.

They came to the country to colonize some land. But it turned out that the lands they were going to colonize belonged to the native community of Matagalpa. The lands were not vacant or anything of the kind; they had an owner. In order to locate these foreigners there, the Indians were moved out and their lands taken away. They had to go off to a very mountainous region where subsistence was harder. They told me that one day when the lady's husband, along with some other people, had gone into the mountains to shuck corn or prepare the ground for planting, and she was resting in a hammock on the porch of the house, some Indians came—I was told at the time that they were savage Indians—and with machetes attacked the person in the hammock and slashed her. I said I didn't believe those people were savage Indians, but that they didn't know she was a woman, that all they knew was that the person was a Dane who had taken away their land and they were undoubtedly defending themselves.

This, of course, cost me a punishment, and the inevitable comments on my "bad inclinations." I remember that then an old woman in the house who was in charge of taking care of us said: "It's what I told you, child, this girl isn't going to turn out well. And that," she said, "with all the care I took in not letting her see a pig killed or even a chicken . . ."

According to her, if we saw an animal slaughtered we were going to acquire wicked feelings. And when they were about to kill an animal, they'd take us far away so we wouldn't hear the squeals of the pigs being slaughtered. But even so she used to complain that in spite of all the care she took of me, I didn't have good feelings because I considered it fair that the Indians had attacked that lady with their machetes.

The point is, I didn't find it fair that a Danish lady should be wounded with machetes, but that I did find it fair that the Indians defended themselves against being plundered. The other Danish families left the country; I don't know what they did; the truth is that the Indians didn't just stay with their arms crossed, and they did fight for the right to their lands. I only met that one Danish family. I don't know if there were more in other mountainous regions of the country, or in the same department, but that family stayed there and the lady still has her scars, a sign of the rebellion of the Matagalpa Indian and of the struggle for the right to their lands that went on for a long time.

"I remember one peasant . . ."

I remember one peasant who had lived on the plantation for

many years; he was a kind of settler. His name was Martin. He was a very old man; ever since I can remember he was there on the plantation. Martin worked almost as a slave, because though it's true my grandparents had paternalistic relationships with the peasants, which made them seem less bad or less despotic than others, at bottom they exploited the peasant as much as any other planter did.

I never saw one peasant who protested or who raised his voice, as might have been done with anyone else who did not have such a paternal relationship with them. That is to say, it was worse. They were godparents to the peasants' children, gave them clothes to go away with and get married in when they had to marry, and all this humiliated the peasant even more, and he lived an even more humiliated life, if you will—less independent from the ranch house.

We liked this particular peasant a great deal because he was an old man, and he always enjoyed coming to the ranch house at night to play his guitar and tell us a lot of stories. After a day's work we always used to gather there at about six o'clock in the evening and sit down and talk. The house had a porch and some chairs where we would sit down for a cup of coffee or tea and cake . . . And next to that porch there was a kind of garage, not really a garage, but a place, open on both sides, with a roof.

The peasants used to come to play a serenade with violins and everything . . . When we were gathered together and alone, the oldest ones, those who lived there on the farm, would sit down and we, the little ones, would start talking with them. They would tell us stories and sing and spend a while there with us . . .

Then this Martin would come along; come straight over and tell us stories, stories of the countryside. He told us about ghosts, stories "of the road" as we called them. About *seguas** and the *cadejo*. A *cadejo* is an animal, like a magic animal that looks like a dog. It doesn't exist but the peasants believe in it and say it scares us and that we like to be told that kind of a story.

Then, especially when the older people of the house went away, we used to go to the camp. We didn't like to stay alone in the

---

* A *segua* is an enchanted woman, as in the Mexican legend "La llorana." She goes out at night and lets out a whistling sound.

house—it was very big—so we went to the camp and the peasants always played their guitars and sang and told stories . . .

The camp was a kind of large room where the coffee pickers lived during the coffee harvesting season, and where the permanent workers who had no families lived. It was horrible, really inhuman conditions: great big rooms stuffed with people, unhealthy, without even minimal facilities . . . And yet we were taught to see as quite natural that human beings were living in these places . . . The workers with families lived in houses, shacks, elsewhere. Shacks just as bad.

In those days Martin was accustomed to taking us to the camp. And he showed us wild fruits, animal caves . . . Martin's only vice was drinking, and my grandfather gave him a good scolding when he was drinking, without realizing that Martin was a man as old as he, or maybe older, and that he deserved respect . . . possibly he didn't think he should be like that. One day Martin was walking toward the house and fell down. They ran to see what was the matter, and he was dead. He must have had a heart attack, a stoppage of breathing and circulation . . . Nobody even knew that Martin had heart trouble. It affected us a great deal because he was our friend.

I must have been eleven or twelve when this happened. My mama told us that Martin died of a heart attack because of so much vexation given to him on the plantation. For Martin had worked as hard as my grandfather or maybe harder and in worse conditions. But he never even had time to realize he was sick because he had no way of going to a doctor.

"Wait, my husband is asleep . . ."

The life of a peasant, especially in the north, is very hard. They live worse than animals. I found out about cases of peasant women dying in childbirth, and I knew of a case, for example, of a peasant woman who died of childbirth on a cattle ranch. They have pure-bred cattle on that ranch, very expensive, and every time a cow is about to calve they bring the veterinarian from the city. The birth of a calf is quite an occasion.

Once one of the cows was giving birth and they brought the

veterinarian and there were a lot of people waiting for the birth. And at the same time in a house right there in the valley where the ranch was, a woman died as a result of delivering her child. After giving birth she got an infection and died. They found out at the plantation house, only after the cow had had her calf, that the woman, who worked there, had died. Because the landowners couldn't attend to anybody until the cow had calved.

The companion of that peasant woman who died in childbirth said to me, when he was telling me this, that if they had even taken her to the veterinarian who was attending the cow, maybe his wife and son wouldn't have died. The child died before the mother.

Another case, and on the same farm, was that of a man who in the pruning—in the cleaning up of the coffee plantation—cut himself in the leg with his machete. Two days went by in which he wasn't given any penicillin, absolutely none. The leg was becoming inflamed and he had lost a lot of blood. The plantation valley was right opposite the ranch house and the landowners didn't even know that the peasant was injured.

When someone did find out by chance—he found out not so much by chance but because he was asked to do something for the man who had a high fever and was delirious, and he went and saw the state the peasant was in and said he couldn't do anything; that it was up to the landowner, up to the owner of the plantation. He said he couldn't take him to a hospital, to a waiting room, because they almost always die there. They take them there and to the hospitals; the medical treatment is so bad in the cities, especially the medical treatment given to the so-called "indigents," that the peasants and people who go there usually die of infections. Because of the lack of cleanliness.

Then the wife of the peasant went to see the landowner and came back and told the person that the landowner's wife had told her the man was sleeping. She had said to her: "Wait, my husband is asleep . . ." Then this person who had some family connection with the owner of the plantation went and woke him up. He obliged the landowner to take the peasant to a doctor. Only in this way . . . They have no dispensary, not even an aspirin or a drug to take away the pain . . .

" . . . the system obliges them to exploit each other . . . "

I went to school in the city and returned on weekends and during vacations to the countryside. The peasant children never went to school because in the plantation valley there was no school, unless the parents were able to afford to send them to an even more remote place where there was one. But the problem was that those families need their children's work too. So the children had to work at farm chores, some in the plantation house, others in the fields themselves, helping their parents to carry out their tasks—by agreement, as they called it there.

The head of the family takes a parcel of land, agreeing to clear and plant it in a set time—for that they pay him. Now, he has to look for people to help him carry out that work, and it is up to him to finish in the least time possible, so the pay is higher. No, not so the pay is higher, but simply to be able to survive. That's the truth. He resorts to his wife, his children, his mother, his grandmother, to whoever is at hand to do the work. The children work—ten, even seven year old children work like adults. They are given a machete and made to clear the land.

The only children who sometimes went to school were the children in the house, that is, those who had a direct connection with us, those who accompanied us in our play. These children were sent to school. My grandmother sent them.

But there too the system took charge of maintaining the difference between the classes . . . There was the case of a child adopted by my grandfather; he sent him to the same school where my brothers and sisters went. But he was undoubtedly sent when he was already a big boy and he didn't feel comfortable, didn't want to be in that school . . . Undoubtedly being with other young ones from the city—he was a peasant with a way of talking and dressing that was totally different—he felt uncomfortable. And he asked them not to send him to that school any more. But he did learn to read and write.

Besides, more than anything it was for the people living in the house. They were people who later were going to work for them as messengers, note keepers—people who had to learn to read and write to be able to organize the work of the plantation. Permitting them a half-baked education responded completely to the interests of the landowners.

There in the camp the children were exploited at great length. Even their mothers, out of necessity, rented them out like objects. I knew of a girl who was being hired out by her mother to another family to haul water, because she was so small that all she could do was bring pails of water, and even that with much difficulty. And she wasn't given even a fifth of the salary her work was bringing in; her mother took it all . . .

She was a woman with many children so she hired them out to other families, also peasants but a little more well-to-do than she, to care for children and so on. The nature of the system obliged them to exploit one another. Those little girls were being deformed from that time on. In that system children are being deformed at an early age. Because of the type of relationship existing in the home, they are an object, a "thing," and if they don't help out economically in the house, they are hindrances. It's an objective matter. All this prevents their being able to go as far as to develop themselves or aspire to go to a school, to study . . . From when they are very small they are contributing with their physical labour to the maintenance of the family.

". . . where for the first time I could distinguish social differences . . ."

Part of my childhood was spent in a mine also. There my papa worked as a technical electrician or something like that. This mine was in the department of Matagalpa; it was called "The Queen" and was once a very active mine. Now it's abandoned. They used to extract ore from it.

It may have been in this place where for the first time I could distinguish social differences. In this mine there were places for technicians and employees of some importance, and other places for the miners. This division reached these people's children since the play areas, as well as the school, were separated. Rather, it should be said that there were play areas and a school only for the children of the technicians, because the miners' children had to play in the ditches and anywhere they were allowed. And they didn't have any school. From those times I remember the great social division that existed, even among the technicians and engineers themselves and the employees of the bureaucracy. There was a little grass-covered square bordered by the houses of the people who occupied a higher position in the hierarchy, and as the social status descended the houses were farther away from the little square until they reached those of the miners in the hollow.

Nicaragua has gold, silver, and copper mines, and now lead and zinc have been added. Nevertheless they are not important industries with regard to the country's holdings. These were working mines and are functioning as enclaves of North American companies. What they produce is taken out directly by the companies having the concessions for exploitation. Just like the banana plantations and the exploitation of lumber from the Atlantic coast . . .

". . . I realized that this thing, war, was not so easy . . ."

As a child, what was my idea of what my life was going to be? Well, when I was exactly five years old, in 1948—I was born in 1943—it was three years since the war had ended and in those days I was very much afraid of the war. People were still listening and commenting, and my mama told me about the Nazi concentration camps.

The Nicaraguans were not fighting with their country, that is to say, the Nicaraguans who were fighting were doing it with the North American army. And my mother used to talk to us about the concentration camps, told us how the Nazis murdered women and children, and what a concentration camp was like . . . At home we listened a lot to foreign radio programs. It was at that time that I developed a real fear of fascism and I was constantly thinking: when will another war come? And I don't know why, but I thought that the first to die in a war would be the children. Undoubtedly I couldn't imagine how a child could take part in a war if he weren't dying.

So perhaps that didn't let me see beyond the moment when a new war might come, and I had no exact idea of what I would

become. Till I was older—I was about ten—when I realized that
this thing, war, was not so easy . . .

"The nuns told us that marriage was woman's cross . . ."

When I was ten years old I planned to be a nun. And I asked the
nuns to accept me as a novice in the school. The nuns did accept
me, but then my papa protested because he said I was too young for
them to inculcate me with their ideas. But it was natural that I
should think that way because in the religious schools where they
train nuns the question of sex, marriage and all that was taboo.
They made us look on marriage as something to be undergone with
resignation, and we were inculcated with the idea, and induced to
think of the possibility of becoming nuns.

The nuns told us that marriage was woman's cross; that life was
a Calvary and that in a Calvary everybody bears her cross.
Woman's cross was marriage and she had to bear it.

As for my parent's marriage, well, during my childhood the
relationship between my mama and papa didn't seem to us like a
bad thing. The problem at home sharpened at the time my father
was militarized. Before that, with all his faults, he was not a
partisan of Somoza and he didn't present great problems . . . Nor
did we give him occasion to have any problems with us. My mama
knew more or less how to carry out her activities so that he
wouldn't get upset. In those days we were not aware that there was
anything wrong, although undoubtedly there must have been. But
we were living a life very much on the fringe of domestic problems
. . .

As I was telling you, I wasn't planning on marriage as part of my
future—in spite of the fact that it is the traditional future of women
in my country—because for me marriage was the very image of
terror. On the other hand, my papa contributed a lot, because he
told me that a woman marries for the sole purpose of suffering,
and since I was his oldest daughter he didn't want me to suffer and
he did want me to study. He wanted me to be an electrical
engineer like himself.

It's strange. It's undoubtedly a complicated matter. My papa
has never agreed to his daughters' marrying. He wanted to have a

heap of old maids in the house. My papa seems to have been born a century too late. He was even very satisfied that most of his children were females—there are nine of us. Nine out of eleven. According to his mentality a woman is something that can be dominated, something he could do what he wanted with . . . He couldn't conceive of our leading an independent life, deciding for ourselves the day we'd marry, or if we weren't going to marry, how we'd live our life . . .

He always wanted us to study, but what he never wanted was for us to marry or have relations with boys. He gave me some freedom, even letting me play with boys; I played with my brothers' friends but he never imagined that we girls might come to have a boy friend. And when we really did have one, it was scandalous.

I had my first boy friend when I was sixteen. Maybe in that sense I acted a little late in comparison with my other girl friends and relatives. In my family people usually marry very young—at sixteen, seventeen or eighteen. I got a bachelor degree without having married, and I had my first boy friend when I was sixteen. I was backward in this respect. I didn't usually go to parties. Since I was very little, I've never gone to birthday parties; I didn't like them.

I was shy. And besides, I didn't know what to do at a birthday party. I couldn't get into the mood, and I had more fun being with children, playing ball instead of with dolls. Really, ever since I was a little girl I didn't see any difference between the sexes, and besides, my relationship with the peasant children was a landowner-peasant one. At bottom I must not have seen them as equals.

Rather, my shyness dated from adolescence. When I was a child I was almost always in the countryside. I had very few friends in the city, and they were friends of my brothers and sisters. But my shyness came from the nuns' school.

Besides, I felt physically inferior to the other girls in my class. The city girls in my class were white, blond, tall and had blue eyes—like my cousins. And I was dark-skinned, short, dark-haired, with brown eyes, and so in a certain sense I felt different from the others. I thought I was ugly.

It was probably also owing to the fact that in my adolescence, when I was twelve or thirteen, there were money problems at home, and I realized I couldn't be given the luxuries that other girls in my class had. Really I don't know . . . In the capitalist system there are so many circumstances in which a girl or boy comes to feel inferior . . .

". . . *we were always mentally bound to my grandparents' plantation . . ."*

There in Matagalpa, in the primary grades, we always spent the week at school and doing things totally subordinate to it. We were not allowed to go out for a walk until we had done all our school work. We were too many children, so we were kept practically locked up among ourselves. We had a very large house in the city, and that was where we used to play. The house had a lot of rooms and two patios, the main one and a large one behind the house where we could ride horses; that one had palm trees in it. We used to spend the whole day playing, that is, the part of the day when we were not in school.

But we were always mentally bound to my grandparents' plantation and were always waiting for the day when we'd go there. We felt freer there than in the city. In the city the usual thing to do was to go to the movies. We weren't allowed to go during the week except when there were cowboy films or films made for children. They were usually shown on Saturday afternoons.

And stories were banned for us; only on weekends could we read stories or see those Walt Disney cartoons—*paquines*, we called them. In that sense my mama was very strict. Although I don't remember that she ever spanked us, but she certainly did punish us by not letting us go to the movies for a month . . .

My papa practically never interfered in the forming of our character. It was always my mama. Those things are the concern of the mother, not the father, except on very rare occasions when he took some part. In that sense my mother had complete freedom.

I know I have one half sister, older than we are and born to a lady when my papa was very young, before he married my mother. I never met her but I found out about her when I was grown. And after my mother's death I had one half brother whom I never met either.

And my sisters and brothers? My oldest brother is a landowner, also a rancher dedicated to cattle raising and the cultivation of coffee. The youngest, a year younger than I, is a technician in milk products, works in a laboratory—*la Prolacsa*, belonging to the multinational Nestle Company. He works there in the northern part of the country for all of Central America. And my sisters? Most of them are already married. They're housewives. Two of their husbands are also landowners. They live in the city of Matagalpa. Another married a Nicaraguan who has North American citizenship and is a member of the North American army. They live in the United States. Another works in the United States and the rest are unmarried and study in Matagalpa . . .

1955 - 1965

"Nicaragua's Atlantic coast has a large percentage of Blacks . . ."

In 1956, before Somoza Garcia's* execution, I went to live with one of my papa's brothers on the Atlantic coast, in the city of Bluefields. There I was able to become aware of the enormous racial discrimination against the black population. Nicaragua's Atlantic coast has a large percentage of Blacks brought in colonial times from Africa as slaves. These people's principal work is in the mining centers, just like the poorer native population.

In the house where I lived there was a black maidservant, a *china*, a children's nurse, charged with taking care of a little daughter of the couple who owned the house. This woman had a salary of thirty *cordobas*—four dollars. For this the woman had to attend to the child, take care of her food, wash and iron for her, care for her clothing, and take her out for walks. After finishing everything having to do with the little girl, she had to do other kinds of work for which she wasn't paid, for example, embroidering, weaving, and even sewing some clothes for the owner of the house.

These tasks occupied the woman until after seven or eight at night, at times until midnight or one in the morning. Once she had to weave far into the night because she wasn't permitted to do it during the day on account of having to take care of the child; she had to weave a white altar cloth because one of the lady's children was going to make her first communion.

It was an altar cloth which, if bought in the street, would have cost her some seven hundred, or perhaps a thousand *cordobas*. A

* Rigoberto Lopez Perez, young revolutionary, executed dictator Somoza Garcia September 21, 1956. Rigoberto killed same day by tyrant's bodyguards.

38

very large one. Yet this woman wove it without receiving any extra salary for it—not even good treatment.

Once when the family was away—the lady of the house and her husband had gone out to have a good time, intending to come home late at night—this woman had to stay by the front door, inside, glued to the door and awake because she was obliged to open it the very instant her employers arrived. The lady of the house didn't like to have to knock.

The woman who owned the house had black blood also, but she felt great disdain toward other blacks. She was a mixture of Chinese, black and white. I remember that once her husband had to go out into the street to fight, to "jump on" a black man because he had had the gall to pass by the sidewalk of his house. The woman wasn't allowed visits from her family because they were black. To be with her mother or brothers and sisters she had to steal out at night far from the house and without her employer's knowledge.

Next to their house was a movie theater, and it was a usual thing for the theater to have some music played before the show went on, so the townspeople could dance to it, in the street or on the sidewalk. Nevertheless, to go to that movie the blacks were not allowed to walk on the sidewalk in front of the lady's house—where I was living—but those "good-for-nothings" had to go into the street and walk there to go to the movie theater, because it bothered the lady to see blacks.

At the time I'm talking about, a Black "dared" to walk past the house on the sidewalk, so she called her husband and made him first beat the Black and then go to the police and have them arrest the man for having used the sidewalk in front of their house.

As for me, they wouldn't let me make friends with the black population, with black children. To be able to chat with the woman who worked in the house, or find out about her problems, I had to do it secretly.

That woman didn't even have a place in the house to lay her head. She had to put a mattress—or whatever could serve as a mattress, old clothes and such—in some corner of the house. Once she had to sleep outside, in a kind of open-air garret.

This woman had some training; she had graduated as a bilingual secretary, but because of the high unemployment, because of the lack of any possibility of finding work in that particular region—which is totally isolated from the rest of the country, accessible at that time only by plane, and now by a highway from the city of Rama—and given the situation then in which all the people lived, that woman, in spite of all her education, had to work as a servant and suffer all the humiliation dealt out to her by the lady of the house.

" . . . a common spectacle that horrifies the bourgeosie . . . "

Among the Bluefields population, especially among the people who are working or did work in the mines, the amount of tuberculosis is frightful. I believe that some ten or twelve years ago, maybe a little more, the official statistics showed that 80 per cent or more of the population had tuberculosis.

And this problem was not confined to the Atlantic coast alone, but was generalized throughout the country. By the year 1960 or 1961, in a little Managua school at the Salvadorita Sugar Plantation, attended by middle class children, the children of one classroom were given the tuberculosis test. And the horrified teacher told me that for every one of the children in that classroom, the tests were positive.

My sister was in that class. This didn't mean that every one of the children actually had the disease but that all were susceptible to it. This was a few years ago, when the economic situation was not as bad as it is now, and among middle class people who could afford the luxury of eating meat once or twice a week, and having milk—at least the children. From this you can imagine the situation of the children of the workers or peasants who have a diet totally lacking in proteins and vitamins. These people live on black coffee, sometimes beans or whatever they can find.

I remember that during those years—or maybe a little before—there was an increase of tuberculosis in the country. This was when the government closed a hospital for tuberculars. It was closed for lack of funds to run it, or how should I know—but for sure it wasn't closed for lack of sick people or because there was no need for a hospital of this kind.

In Nicaragua it is a very common thing to have tuberculosis. You see people with the disease in the doorways of churches or of big stores. They find themselves obliged to fall back on begging or public charity to be able to eat. Once I saw a tubercular woman die in the atrium of the Matagalpa cathedral. She was spitting up blood and when she vomited, an older daughter, who was also spitting up blood, helped her. Mother, daughter, and a child who was going about with them were all sick with tuberculosis. This is a common spectacle that horrifies the bourgeoisie so much that when they see the sick people they run away. In Nicaragua many tuberculars die on the sidewalks.

Comrades Casimiro Sotelo and Julio Buitrago carried on an investigation on the situation of the Atlantic coast miners, in Bonanza and Siuna. They exposed not only the exploitation the miners suffered but also how they were being killed. Of course not only the mining companies are guilty of this, but also Somoza, who receives annually a certain number of dollars from these companies. At that time it was shown that most of the miners were tubercular due to the bad conditions in the mines, but that the mine doctors hid this fact when they found out about it so that the miner would continue working until he couldn't work any more. Then came the layoffs without vacations or prior notice. It was also discovered that a doctor was offered three hundred dollars a month to color the aspirin tablets so they'd look like vitamin pills.

From the mines and the tuberculars Nicaragua obtains some $20,000 annually in taxes. Gold is taken out of the country in the rough, so there's no way of knowing how much is stolen.

" . . . collective hysteria . . . collective madness . . . "

The country's health problem is really very serious. There are entire regions of the countryside where there's a sickness called night blindness. This sickness is due mainly to malnutrition. A few years ago there were accusations, and it was pointed out by the opposition bourgeois press, that in the peasant population in the northern part of the country—in Matagalpa—in the city of Dario, there were peasants suffering from night blindness because they were fed so poorly. This was denounced as yellow journalism for the purpose of selling newspapers . . . They never did it again, but this problem of night blindness, also cases of collective hysteria, of collective madness, occasioned principally by malnutrition, are common.

About the problem of insanity in the country, a medical student specializing in psychiatry told me that the majority of cases were determined, or aggravated if you will, by bad food. This malady was suffered by people who didn't have a chance to be cured because when they left the hospital, they went right back to their poor nourishment and to work or study scarcely able to eat.

After the earthquake the situation changed, but the trauma caused by the earthquake which affected 100 per cent of Managua's population became worse when the scarcities of life began increasing in cost, when people couldn't even obtain a subsistence diet . . .

A dozen eggs, for example, cost a dollar. A pound of meat cost ten or twelve *cordobas*: almost two dollars. The average salary of a worker never goes beyond ten or twelve *cordobas* a day. And there are people who earn less than that. The population has no opportunity to feed itself, can't feed itself, can't afford to acquire the necessary food to subsist as human beings . . .

"They made him a guard."

After Somoza's assassination in 1956 by Rigoberto Lopez Perez, the situation in the country became even worse, if that's possible. Great repression broke loose. After September 21 the repression flared up again, and an incalculable number of people were taken prisoner. I remember that in those days they arrested a woman from my town, Dona Luz Marina de Alonzo, the wife of Julio Alonzo; a member of the Guard who rose up against the Somozas.

They kept that comrade incommunicado for many days. In those times Rigoberto's mother and sister were captured. There was a lot of terror; nobody knew exactly what was happening. It's my opinion that the most frightening thing was that I didn't know if old Somoza had died—because the government people were saying he was well and already sitting up. It was like a kind of threat . . .

That was when I was really beginning to acquire a true

consciousness, if you will, of the effect the Guard's terror had on the people. I was thirteen then. In those days I began to become acquainted with certain revolutionary literature, for the first time reading Maxim Gorky's *The Mother.*

The situation in my house was becoming difficult. My papa had to sell some property he owned in Matagalpa and move to Managua to work as a television technician. Television had recently entered the country and was owned by the Somoza family, so it turned out to be a bad job. He didn't receive any salary for a year, and to cap it all he was put into the military. They made him a guard. This situation forced the rest of the family to also move to the capital.

" . . . my mama tried to make all her children adopt logical positions . . ."

In Managua my mama impressed upon me the need of my continuing to study at a government institute. I think my mama tried to make all her children adopt logical positions or be militants. But it was doubtless necessary to take into account the way we lived and the disposition of each of us. We had to bear in mind the character of each of us. Moreover my mother's family had to support my other brothers and sisters in religious schools while I went to study at the Institute.

My oldest brother, at the expense of my grandparents, was studying at the Central American School of the Jesuits. And some of my younger sisters were at a nuns' school—also paid for by my grandparents. I remember that some relative of my papa offered to pay my way in that school and that my mama left it up to me. I preferred the Institute. I never wanted to depend on my relatives for money.

All that was very positive. That is where I entered into contact with students—women and men—who came from the lowest social classes. My relationship with them was not the paternalistic relationship of someone living on the plantation, with the rank, if you will, of landowner, and the exploited peasant. It was a relationship of equality.

In regard to political positions I also went ahead a step. During my childhood, my oppositional outlook was conservative. For me, opposition was synthesized in the Conservative Party. But in the country's presidential elections, one wing of the Conservative Party lent itself to playing Somoza's game and went to the elections. The Somozas needed a man who, in exchange for money and a *curul*,* would be ready to bow out in defeat— "overthrown"—and they found that man in the Conservative Party.

In addition to this, there was Rigoberto Lopez Perez's act. He was not a Conservative. I think the difference became clear to me. While a man of the people gives up his life and collects the debt the tyrant owed to the common people—Sandino's assassination— a man of the conservative oligarchy lends himself so the Somoza family can remain in power.

For the Nicaraguan people, then, Rigoberto Lopez Perez signified or represented national dignity. He was a man who had conscientiously confronted one of Sandino's assassins. That was what Rigoberto meant for us. In my house we used to talk about him with a lot of respect, and for me he signified true opposition to the Somozas . . .

I can recall that in my house there was a photo of Rigoberto that they used to show us so we'd recognize him. At the bottom of that photo was a stanza of one of Rigoberto's poems that read: "The flowers of my days will be withered/while the tyrant has blood in his veins." I don't know if I've quoted it correctly, but I don't think I'm mistaken. My mama explained it meant we had to get rid of Somoza.

With the sham elections of 1957, I realized that the Conservatives did no more than be loyal to their tradition. It is the Conservatives who continually ask for Yankee intervention in the country, and it is the Conservatives who have been giving up their political pretensions, supporting and participating in planning the assassination of General Sandino.

---

* *Curul*: a post, a job. A *curulero* sells himself for money or position.

"I heard talk of Darwin . . ."

Toward this time—1957 and 1958—and through my relationships at the Institute, my religious beliefs were being put to the test. I was thirteen or fourteen years old. One day in class the subject was the origin of the planet, and then the professor asked us to explain our opinions. I must have stood up and said that the world had been created in seven days and that it had been created by God and that men had appeared made out of mud and with a divine breath and . . . and everything else one learns in a religious school. My professor smiled and the other students who came from lay schools and had not been given that kind of an education laughed at me. This disturbed me a lot.

I went to the priest and told him that because I couldn't explain it all, everybody laughed at me, and why didn't he tell me how the world was created? Then the priest told me I was following very wicked ways, that I was surely going to come to a bad end because those were things that must not be doubted; that's how it was and if I was going to want to explain a lot of things I'd reach the moment when I'd become proud and haughty and deny God. It was then I told him I would definitely not go to church any more, that I was never again going to say what they had taught me because that was what made people laugh at me, and it was all a lie.

My professor had given an explanation which was far from being a materialistic explanation. He put forth the theory of a French mathematician, Laplace, which wasn't correct either, but was more logical and alongside the explanation I had been given, well, it was closer to the truth.

So began my breaking away from religion . . .

For me it was a very difficult question, because I was a person much attached to the Church, was a catachist, taught the catachism to the other children, did one good deed a day, went to communion, went to daily mass, prayed the rosary and observed all the religious practices . . . I did penance, was constantly doing penance because I felt somewhat guilty for the situation of poor children, for a series of ignominious happenings typical of a class society . . .

So it is that in this period I realized that my whole religious "foundation" had nothing to hold onto, had no scientific base. I heard talk of Darwin and of other theories of how the world was created and how man appeared on earth . . .

"Better put this thing under your seat . . . "

At this time my mama was acquainted with some people, probably with the guerrillas headed by General Ramon Raudales who fell in 1958. Maybe that was my first act of conspiracy, no? One of them gave my mama a box containing boots, food and a rifle with telescopic sight to be moved to a place in the camp. At that time there were reserve corps on the highway; that's where the buses and all vehicles were stopped, passengers put off and inspections made of the vehicles.

To get a boxful of boots and some food through for the mountain zone was no problem; the problem was getting the rifle through. It hadn't occurred to anybody to take it apart so it could go through undetected in pieces. They delivered it to my mama wrapped in a lined linen bag. My mama called me and explained that there was a rifle there, that it had to be taken somewhere else and that if she took it they would very probably find it. Then she asked me if I dared take it . . . I told her yes.

This was a measure of my mama's desire to participate, for in spite of the risk I was going to run, it didn't make any difference to her. I went in a public conveyance. The assistant or driver of the vehicle—I don't exactly remember—took hold of what I was carrying and of course felt its weight. He asked me what I was carrying. At that moment I didn't think and I told him I was carrying some candles for a first communion.

It was absurd to take a few candles wrapped up in a linen bag—and besides, the weight itself—so the driver realized that it couldn't be candles, because of the weight and the way the thing was wrapped, and then he said to me: "Better put this thing under your seat and when the first reserve corps comes, be asleep."

I went all the way acting as if I were asleep, and when the bus stopped everybody got off and I stayed there asleep. Then the driver told the guard that was going to make the inspection: "Wait, I'm going to wake the girl; she's my responsibility." But the guard said: "No, let that young one sleep." And they didn't make me get off and didn't lift up the seat. They were even looking underneath the bus and everything. That was how we got the rifle through.

Later, my mama made me see how, by staying calm, a person can do anything . . . I had a lot of luck, because the driver could have been an "ear," but the repudiation of the regime by the Nicaraguan people is generalized. The sectors lending support to the regime are very few. And this demonstrates it . . .

I remember that the townspeople were saying that Raudales was the "tiger's skin" of the Somozas. General Ramon Raudales headed the guerrillas in 1958; Heriberto Reyes took part with him.These two are Sandinist veterans who kept the Sandino struggle alive. Students participated in this guerrilla warfare: I remember Manuel Baldizon. Manuel was from my town. He studied in Mexico. After Raudales was killed, Manuel took part in the Chaparral guerrilla movement, in 1959. Comrade Carlos Fonseca also took part, and was wounded. These two movements were backed by the people, although the oligarchy tried to channel them in its favour . . .

" . . . not permitting Ernesto Cardenal's books to enter the country is reaching the point of being ridiculous."

In 1957-1958 I took part in street struggles for the first time. I can recall great popular demonstrations, in which students participated, against the arrival of Milton Eisenhower who had been invited by the University. There were also demonstrations demanding the release of comrade Tomas Borge.

In 1959 I became acquainted with some of my mama's friends and I remember that they brought to the house books like *The Holy Family* and *The Origin of the Family, Private Property and the State*, and for the first time I heard them talk about *Das Kapital*.

I have to emphasize my contact with these books because in those days, in 1959 and before, to get hold of a Marxist book was an extraordinary event. *The Mother* had been kept by my mama ever since she was seventeen or eighteen. The others were smuggled into the country.

Ignorance of this kind of literature was so great that the person

who loaned me the book told me, laughing, how the customs
officials had seen the book called *The Holy Family* and had let it
pass, naturally assuming it was a religious book.

At present there are many opportunities to obtain revolutionary
literature, including the classics. Although from time to time the
Security Office carries out inspections of the bookstores, or simply
doesn't let books into the country. In this sense not permitting
Ernesto Cardenal's* books to enter the country is reaching the
point of being ridiculous. Of course this is understandable,
because the regime has been kept in power thanks to the political
ignorance of the people, maintained at bayonet point and with the
help of Yankee dollars.

" . . . I realized that men didn't devour girls . . . "

That first year at the Institute, as I told you, was very important
for me. When I told my mama what happened about my religious
beliefs, she said that the Church made a mistake in not explaining
things well, and that surely many of the things the Catholic Church
said were not true, and that given the way I was developing and
finding out how things were, I'd gradually understand. And she
was sorry the Church was like that.

I learned something else very important in the Ramirez Goyena
Institute, how to get along with persons of another class in a totally
different atmosphere than the one that shaped me. And on the
other hand I learned to deal with men as companions. They were
my study companions and I realized that men didn't devour girls
and that I didn't have to see them as something different or see
myself as something different from them.

After the demonstrations to free Tomas Borge, and the arrival
of Milton Eisenhower, the students taking part in them suffered
repression, especially those in the institutes. The form this took
was to forbid them to matriculate by claiming they were
undisciplined or that there was no room.

There was also the fact that I refused to accept Christian
postulates, a Christian conception of the world, or Christian social

* Ernesto Cardenal is a Nicaraguan poet, Catholic priest and Marxist revolutionary.

norms any more. We had a professor who was a priest, who taught us "morals." So I devoted myself to bothering him continually, that is, I didn't have any basis for discussing things with him but rejected everything the priest told us, and that gave rise to a tense situation between us.

Then the following year when I was going to matriculate in the Institute—my second year—they asked my papa to commit himself to signing a paper saying I wouldn't participate in any political activity or talk about religion inside the Institute. This proved to my papa that I had gone beyond being against Somoza, and that I was participating in things even my brothers had no part in.

I was taken out of the Institute. And as punishment I was sent to a nuns' school. It was a very, very difficult matter for me because the nuns told the other girl students that I came from an institute, and I was looked upon as a strange being. The girls came to ask me what was done in an institute . . .

They considered this matter of being among men as something totally abnormal and grotesque. With this darkening of the picture the only thing they do is create morbidity in the students, and they imagine that the Institute students never go as far as to study, only indulge in I don't know what kind of depravity and . . . And they felt defrauded when I told them education was the main thing, that it demanded more of us, and that even at fifteen I'd never had a boy friend.

"They said 'the devil always stands between two people.' "

This year was very difficult for me. Not only because I was in a nuns' school, but because I knew that every month I had to pay a very large sum of money. I think they must have paid about a hundred dollars a month on me alone, and this meant many deprivations for the others. Besides, it was at a time of great political activity.

On one occasion the nuns planned a spiritual "retreat." This is a Catholic activity for young people and adults. There was a priest there who gave sermons and you had to meditate. He talked about morality, etc. At the end of the retreat I remember that one student stood up and said she wanted to talk to us about her own

problem . . . She started to tell us her parents were members of a
club—I don't remember if it was the Lions' or the Rotary—and she
had never done anything to get in the way of this, but after the
"retreat" she would commit herself to do all she could to work
against it.

I was surprised because I knew that those institutions were
instruments of the bourgeoisie for the purpose of carrying out
"social activities" to conceal activities not so social. I asked what
the problem was and they explained that those clubs were like the
Masons, that married couples changed partners and that
unmarried people went to bed with married people . . . In short, a
whole, immoral and horrible picture. This gives you some idea of
the deliberate vagueness preached by priests and nuns, the kind of
moulding which one receives there, and the effect I could have on
them—I, who came accused of being a "communist" . . .

Something else that exemplifies the damage suffered by a
student in these schools is the following. A nun told us she was
very innocent because when she was sixteen or seventeen her
mama or some relative of hers was expecting a baby and she was
always looking up at the sky to see the child when it fell . . . We
knew it wasn't like that. The surest thing is that at that age she had
known things too, but with this story she tried to establish an
equality between "ignorance" and "virtue."

Life in these boarding schools was intolerable. When we were
going to take a bath they ordered us to do it with a cotton garment
reaching to our knees, slit up the sides to our waists so we could
soap ourselves. The nun in charge of the bathroom told us that
when soaping ourselves we should start to sing, mentally, and that
we should never look at our bodies—to avoid "bad thoughts."

She also forbade conversation between two girls alone; we had to
do so in a group and out loud. They said "the devil always stands
between two people."

Keeping an eye on classes not given by the nuns themselves
topped it off. We had two lay professors; one taught biology, and I
can't recall the specialty of the other. They were older men but I
don't know what the nuns thought of them because both classes
had observers: a nun seated at the door "seeing and hearing"
what those professors said or did. It was also the custom to cross

out passages in books—"reproduction" for example, in the biology book.

The repression in these study centers is beyond belief. Once they expelled three pupils—boarding pupils—in the fifth year of their BA degree. First they isolated them from the rest of the pupils . . . Nobody knew what was happening and then they called in their papas. It was an impressive thing to see how they left the school in the midst of deep silence and visibly ashamed. The nuns told us we mustn't talk with them when they returned to school—the expulsion was temporary—because they were "bad girls." It wasn't hard for us to discover their crime; the nuns found out they had boy friends and were writing to them—and to cap it all they were smoking. Those students must have been eighteen or nineteen . . .

So I spent the year there but my papa lifted the punishment the next year. That year marked a very important event in the life of the student movement. The year 1959. The Guard had massacred a guerrilla band in El Chaparral. Because of this event the university students went out to demonstrate on July 23. That demonstration was put down not only savagely, but cowardly—from behind. Four university students were killed and hundreds of townspeople injured. July 23 is one of the days characterizing the Somoza regime.

"Now it's a sure thing!"

In that period, probably influenced by the truimph of the Cuban Revolution, I gained an awareness that, faced with so much violence, it's necessary to respond with violence. Accounts of the Somoza crimes and comments on the guerrilla movements, happening between 1958 and 1959, were the daily bread in my house.

In November of 1959 the Guard assassinated my first cousin Chale Haslam. He died after having supported himself in the mountains for some nine months. The guerrilla band of which Chale was a member was characterized by being largely composed of peasants; nevertheless, it suffered from the same sickness of all the movements of those days, that is, it had no conception of a correct strategy.

I knew this guerrilla group very intimately, and I realized they came to an end principally for this reason; they thought they could throw out the regime by themselves alone. They didn't understand and I'm almost sure they didn't even know they needed a political vanguard.

Those were years of great political activity in the country, an age of great hopes, days when many exclaimed: "Now it's a sure thing!"

". . . Sandino was the one who captured a North American flag and sent it . . . to an anti-imperialist congress."

In the first months of 1960 the Patriotic Youth of Nicaragua (JPN) was organized, and it was there that I took my first steps as a militant. When I began to serve in the JPN, my participation had another meaning; until 1960 I was a co-worker with my mama, but afterward the roles changed and then I took part in one of my mama's most involved schemes. In my environment it wasn't well regarded that women should be politically militant, much less in an organization like the JPN which showed itself to be in accord with the revolution and stated that socialism was the solution. So that I could attend the meetings she invented "visits" she had to make, and in that way we could go out at night. I took off to the meeting and she waited for me on a street corner or in some other place.

The JPN was too big an organization and because of its class composition was unable to lead the revolution even though there were popular elements in its ranks. Later, some of those comrades went into the Sandinist Front. JPN was a petty bourgeois organization and that was why it disappeared.

I believe that if at the time there had been a political organization capable of channeling all the activity and all the enthusiasm of the JPN, that organization might have performed the role of intermediate organization wonderfully well. But in those days the organized revolutionary movement was in diapers, was taking its first steps . . .

In Patriotic Youth I met comrade Jose Benito Escobar, who at present is serving in the Sandinist Front, and I met other proletarian comrades like him, and I understood the Sandino struggle better. The romantic vision of the semi-literate Sandino who was courageous enough to confront the Yankees . . . I realized then that Sandino had an entire concept of the reasons for his struggle, and could distinguish his allies from his enemies perfectly well, that his army was proletarian and practicing proletarian internationalism, that Sandino was the one who captured a North American flag and sent it . . . to an anti-imperialist congress, in Frankfurt in 1929.

In JPN I worked under the orders of comrade Julio Buitrago. Julio was sixteen years old then, but he was already outstanding in his military skills, his ability to command, the stability and rectitude of character that distinguished his whole life, even more so at the moment of confronting the Guard. In the fight when much later he was assassinated . . .

" . . . with the cry of A Free Country or Death . . . *"*

July 23, 1960, a year after the massacre of July 23, 1959, the country's student movement, together with the popular forces, with all sectors of the people, organized demonstrations to commemorate those four student comrades.

On the morning of July 23, 1960 the students and the Nicaraguan people had been summoned to a Mass in the chapel of Managua's General Hospital. Nine days before the Mass, guards of honour had been placed in Leon, right where the students had been massacred. That honour guard was composed of students, townspeople and professional people who opposed the regime. They stood guard all day and all night.

The mothers of the fallen also participated. Impromptu meetings took place in the principal neighbourhoods, in the schools, outside of institutes and in the streets, at any corner where there were a great many people, or at factory exits . . . A student or a worker would stop and with the cry of *A Free Country or Death!* attract the people's attention and then take the floor, explaining the why and wherefore of the repression against those students, for it wasn't a casual or isolated question but a question of the conditions of life in the country.

When July 23 arrived, the people and students gathered at the General Hospital in Managua. Just as the Mass was beginning, the Guard showed up. Police arrived in trucks and jeeps. They brought a piece of rubber or a stick—we called it a *tajona*—they used to beat people, to break up the demonstrations . . . I think in other places they're called bludgeons or nightsticks . . .

Those policemen came and attacked all the townspeople and students who were at the hospital. Since the students ran off and scattered all through the hospital and all over the district, they even attacked the sick people in the waiting room. It was a very shocking thing because you could see how they threw the sick people out of their beds and beat them and struck them with the butts of their guns. They even threw tear gas bombs inside the hospital.

We—that is to say, the students—had agreed to be in the street all day, in centrally located places, principally on Roosevelt Avenue, the biggest avenue, since that day it had been decided to change its name to Sandino Avenue. A plaque had been ordered—a street sign.

We stayed in places near there, and every hour, with pre-arranged signals, we went out into the street, rushed into the street, stopped traffic, and distributed flyers on the principal avenues. When the clock struck three in the afternoon, the time when we were going to put up the street sign, there was an enormous number of people mainly from the town, congregated all along the street taking part in stopping traffic and handing out flyers.

This was not done only on that one street but on all the important streets of the city because we wanted to get as many people as possible to Roosevelt Avenue at three in the afternoon. Of course during all this time the Guard was being repressive but they couldn't put an end to the demonstration because the demonstration wasn't concentrated at one single point but was spread among all the people in the vicinity.

Then some townspeople were arrested, beaten and had tear gas fired at them, but the police couldn't stop the demonstration and it lasted all day long until three in the afternoon. At three p.m. a group of us students who knew what was going to happen—other people didn't know why they had been called to Roosevelt Avenue for three o'clock—placed ourselves where Roosevelt Avenue begins, at Republic Square.

We tried to march from Republic Square down Roosevelt to the Roosevelt monument at the Presidential Palace and place the street sign there. When we arrived at the corner of the Gran Hotel, the Guard attacked us by firing into the air and throwing tear gas bombs; we scattered along the bordering streets, but we planned to turn around and pour out again into Roosevelt by way of another street a block ahead of where we had been disbanded. We were demonstrating all the time, with the police pursuing us and trying to prevent our continuing, but we were so many they couldn't stop us.

I remember that on the corner of the Gran Hotel, an enraged guard screamed at some people and students. Then a child of about twelve or thirteen let out a roar when that policeman yelled like that. It seemed like a joke, a child making fun of what he had heard. The policeman became furious and since he didn't know who had made fun of him, he attacked the whole crowd, dealing blows with his gun and firing into the air.

We succeeded in getting to a certain part of Roosevelt, but more and more guards were coming. At any rate, we couldn't reach the Roosevelt monument. It was really a difficult thing; we knew we weren't going to be able to do it, because to get to the Roosevelt monument we first had to go down the whole avenue. In the second place, at a definite moment and before coming to the monument, there is the First Division of Police which is also a prison, and also there is the Military Academy and the Parade Grounds which is a kind of Guard barracks. There are also a lot of reserve corps, because the Roosevelt monument is the Presidential Palace. Objectively, we knew it was impossible, but we wanted to go as far as we could. I think we went more than half way. By that time we were at the block where the police barracks is located. And we put up the street sign.

The demonstration mustn't only be seen in terms of the Guard's repression. All along the route there were meetings; the comrades climbed to the top of the highest buildings, started making speeches, and this was done at different points along the way with the object of attracting the attention of the Security and the Police.

I recall that in San Antonio Church, three or four blocks from Roosevelt Avenue, there was also something going on. I don't remember if it was a Mass or . . . what I do remember is that the people had agreed to meet there at a definite time.

The Guard came too. We took some stones that were in the street—some repair work was being done—and answered the Guard's shots and tear gas with them. At that point we succeeded in surrounding a guard. The guard thought we were going to beat him, even kill him. He was in the hands of a great many students and it was impressive to see how, when finding himself without the other guards and surrounded by students, he started to cry and handed over his Garand rifle.

It was an impressive and unpleasant picture. He was a very small guard, a peasant, and when he saw he couldn't fire at the students because of being surrounded by so many, he felt powerless and lost all the ferocity he had had. He handed over his Garand rifle to some of us, and said to us: "Boys and girls, we're brothers and sisters, we're also townspeople, don't kill me!"

Then a student comrade told him we were not killing the Guard, we had no reason to kill the Guard, if we were throwing stones at them it was because they were firing their Garands. Now that he saw he couldn't kill us, he no longer insulted us as he had been doing before.

We made way for him and let him go. When he was in the street we called him back and returned his Garand. And we told him that now that he was in a position to shoot, he should try it, but he didn't. Probably because of our attitude and our conversation with him. We explained to him why we were struggling, and how the Guard—maybe not he personally, but certainly other guards—had fired at the student demonstration, a peaceful demonstration, and had fired behind our backs and killed some students, wounded children and also killed townspeople. We told how we were constantly attacked by them, and had never gone to a demonstration with a gun.

Then the guard told us he knew we were right and he understood us, but they were orders and it wasn't his fault. The guilty ones were the officers and the country's rulers, because he realized, he told us, that for 180 *cordobas*—the salary of a common guard at the time—that for 180 *cordobas*, he was earning the enmity of the people and could even die. The officers who were earning good wages and living well, those men weren't running the risk of dying in a demonstration, or being taken prisoner by the people, because they weren't "going around" with the people, he said. They had nothing to do with the townspeople. They couldn't suffer the consequences of the hate the people felt, the scorn the Nicaraguans felt toward the Guard . . .

Also at another time there was the case of a guard who was isolated from the rest of the squad and hid behind a vehicle. It's nauseating, isn't it? It's repugnant to see how guards, when they're in a squad, insult mothers and young women and beat male demonstrators. Without their Garands or without the rest of the squad, they practically turn into mice. Some of them lose . . . lose all their courage, all their bravery.

That same day, it could have been four o'clock—or before, no exact time—at one of the moments when the Guard was scattering we gathered on the square again, at the foot of the cathedral steps. A student appeared at the cathedral and told us there was a couple going to be married and that the people were very elegant; it seemed it was someone from the government because many state officials were there. At this point a very elegant car drove up, a black one. It belonged to the American Embassy. And a girl dressed as a bride got out—we were at the edge of the steps leading to the cathedral door—a high society girl.

We barricaded the door, told her we wouldn't allow her to marry or have a wedding party that day. Then she said to us from the car: "Boys, I'm a Nicaraguan; let me get married."

A comrade then asked her why she came in the American Embassy car. She explained she was going to marry a member of the Embassy staff, an Embassy attache. She was told we weren't going to let her have a fiesta with a Yankee that day . . .

But the girl started to cry and the Guard near the cathedral came firing. It was then decided to allow her to get married, but not with the customary bourgeois pomp. A comrade took her up the steps. She went into the cathedral on the arm of a student, still crying.

Later we found out that the best-man at the wedding was Somoza. At least that was what we were told. The fact is, she was a member of the bourgeoisie and while the townspeople were being massacred by the Guard, she was marrying an attache of the American Embassy and trying to have us treat her like a Nicaraguan.

The priests of the church shut the door on us. And the Guard started firing at us. We were practically defenseless. Some comrades went up to the Embassy car, turned it over and set it on fire. That day there were squads—that's what we called small groups of three or four student and worker comrades together—scattered all over the city on the main thoroughfares, especially where there was the most traffic. The American Embassy cars, the Guard cars, or cars whose license plates begin with the number 15,000 were set on fire. An enormous quantity of cars burned up. It was very hard to restrain the townspeople.

What was done was to try to restrict the burning of cars to government vehicles or those of the American Embassy. 15,000 was the first five digits on the Security agents' license plates. Of course afterward they stopped using a uniform series of numbers on their plates but at that time they used the figure 15,000. Every car bearing that license plate number belonged to a guard, a high ranking guard, or a Security agent.

That day too—I was told this by a person who participated in one of the squads—there was a very elegant car with a license plate beginning with 15,000. When they were about to turn it over they saw there was a woman in it, and she was lying down on the seat and said to them, crying: "Don't do anything to me; I'm the stepmother of . . ." And she named a comrade, a revolutionary leader.

The comrades didn't burn up the car. As a matter of fact the person who told me this knew her and knew she really was that comrade's stepmother. He told me he was nauseated to see how she made use of that relationship—she is nothing to the comrade, but she tried to take advantange of the pseudo-family relationship to prevent the vehicle's being set on fire. I wonder if she recalled that she was the stepmother of that revolutionary when he was arrested. Nevertheless at that moment she surely did want everyone to realize that the family tie existed.

That day was the first time the Guard beat me; I was arrested but set free on the same street. One of my brothers and I were on Roosevelt Avenue, more or less halfway up. We had managed to get that far by running along the neighbouring streets, avoiding the Guard. When we had gone that far a Guard squad came throwing tear gas bombs and firing into the air. All we did then was sit down on the steps of some establishment on that corner and stay there against the wall.

The squad went past us running and didn't stop. But when they had finished passing, the last guard spotted us. The fellow addressed me first and asked me what I was doing there: "fucking on the street . . ." I told him we were townspeople and that the ones who were fucking were themselves. He grabbed me by the arm and my brother—my younger brother—said to him: "Look, don't take her away. Take me; I'm her brother."

The guard answered: "you're both going to go." And he called another guard who took us, urged on with the butt of his gun, to a vehicle on Roosevelt Avenue. When we arrived there they put my brother into the vehicle and I began to struggle with the police to prevent their putting me in. At that point the head of the patrol arrived; he was an officer who knew my papa and he asked what was happening. I asked him why he was asking; what was happening was that the guards were obeying the orders that officers like himself gave them.

He asked me what I was doing there, and I told him I thought I could walk along the streets like anybody else. This fellow didn't know I was part of the demonstration and told the guard to let me go, that we were the children of a military man, that they were brutes . . .

I said they weren't brutes, just poor ignorant men used by the government and by the officers to repress people. The officer told me I'd better shut up, and if I didn't he was going to have to arrest me. As a matter of fact this fellow, this same officer, arrested me on January 22, 1967. It was his lot to arrest me. Then he was Lieutenant Nicolas Valle Salinas. Now I think he is Colonel Nicolas Valle Salinas.

That day on one of the streets leading into Roosevelt—a block and a half from Roosevelt—when the students were running away from the Guard who were following them, a handicapped student—he had suffered some paralysis since childhood and was using crutches—a boy of fourteen or fifteen, going through his first year at the Ramirez Goyena Institute, was resting on the

sidewalk watching the other comrades run. The passing patrol saw
that he couldn't run because he was on crutches, so they shot him
and killed him. He was comrade Julio Oscar Romero.

The people's fury increased when they saw the crime committed
against that boy. Demonstrations were organized all that day and
night, and people came to stand guard at the place where comrade
Julio Oscar Romero had fallen. He was buried the next day.

That was one of the greatest demonstrations against the regime
of the Somozas. I remember the funeral demonstration—from
beginning to end it was some five or six blocks long . . . The streets
completely filled with people, the people composing slogans,
singing the hymn, singing revolutionary songs, and on every
block, on every corner, there was a student or a worker or a woman
. . . I don't think there was any exploited or oppressed sector of the
Nicaraguan people who were not pronouncing judgement on, or
denouncing that assassination.

The demonstrations continued even up to the twenty-fifth of
July, all over, at factory doors, at the entrances of institutes; there
were enormous demonstrations, great demonstrations, not only by
students but by townspeople, denouncing the massacre of 1959,
denouncing the assassination of comrade Romero.

It was one of the times of greatest activity and street struggles in
the town. That was how important this occasion from July 23 to 25
was for us. Besides, it was somehow linked to the observance of
July 26, the day when meetings were organized in the
neighbourhoods, in the markets, at the doors of factories and in
the schools, to commemorate the Cuban Revolution. Since then,
July 23 has been a day when great popular and student
demonstrations against the regime are organized. July 23 was
recognized as Central American Students' Day by a students'
congress held in Honduras in 1960.

There have been some very good accounts of these events—the
Chaparral massacre and the 1959 and 1960 demonstrations—
written by Comrade Fernando Gordillo,* a Nicaraguan intellectual
revolutionary who lived through the massacre and demonstrations.

The bourgeois accounts have their own purpose. The opposition,
the conservative oligarchy, tried to take away the political aspect of

* He was a member of the FSLN and died on July 25, 1967.

the 1959 demonstration. They accused the regime of barbarity and said it was cruel how they had massacred a fiesta, they said . . . of students! For a long time they tried to lessen the value of it. They said it was the traditional parade of the "downy-chins." University students, at about this time of year, usually went out into the streets in a carnival mood in a parade of what they called the "downy-chins." It was a parade to greet the students who had recently entered the university. But this date coincided with the Chaparral affair, so the demonstration of July 23, 1959, wasn't the traditional parade of the "downy-chins" and wasn't a carnival. It was a protest demonstration against the regime, and that's why it was repressed. They never would have broken up a student carnival; they never had before.

The oppositional bourgeoisie tried to take away its political aspect. Certainly they accused Somoza's regime of the assassination, but when it was a question of the massacre of the students, they never discussed the reasons for it. Instead they repeated that thing about the carnival, that it was criminal how the students had been massacred in their carnival . . . They tried to ignore the real reason, the real reason the students had gone to that demonstration on July 23 1959.

The Chaparral affair was a popular movement that had no connection with the conservative oligarchy or with the opposition bourgeoisie and so they tried to ignore the real reason for the demonstration of July 23, 1959. It is very important to remember that date; those were the first street demonstrations in support of the popular liberation movement of the Nicaraguan people.

". . . we were even going to want to be 'lady' doctors."

In 1960 students also experienced a more subtle repression in the form of the so-called Quintana law. This law held that a student who failed in three subjects lost the whole year. Its objective was to reduce the number of students, especially those who were from the poorer classes.

Maybe to understand this I ought to say that in Nicaragua it's very common these days for the students in the public schools or institutes to faint because of not having eaten breakfast, or fail to be able to carry out their assignments for lack of a notebook, and most of the time they can't study because they don't have the necessary books . . .

Then there are the conditions under which a middle-class or proletarian student has to study; he or she generally has a very large family, irritable parents and a very small house. Almost everything keeps him from studying, from being able to concentrate. The petty bourgeois or bourgeois students does not know these problems. Furthermore, the professors conduct themselves in a different way in an institute than in a private school.

I remember one professor, distinguished in the Goyena for his cruelty to the students. In "La Asuncion" it was another story. The professor there said that a "lady" who studied was doing it because she had a role to play in society, but we weren't anybody, and what we should learn to do was wash, iron, and cook, and the only thing we gained by studying was to "fill our heads with conceit," and we were even going to want to be "lady doctors." When the time for exams came, this same professor didn't even let the proletarian student breathe, while he encouraged the girls and boys of the private schools with smiles and hints . . .

So because of this Quintaná law that tried to limit the right to education for the children of workers, the students threw themselves into the struggle. Nevertheless nothing could be done, and in the year 1963—when I finished my bachelors degree—of some 600 of us who started, 250 obtained the degree. The 350 or more who were unable to finish had to find work, thanks to the Quintana law. No matter what is done for the child of a worker or a peasant, under capitalism he can't study.

" . . . only a workers' party could devote itself to the task of transforming society."

Toward the end of 1960, I joined the Nicaraguan Socialist Youth (JS). When I did maybe I wasn't very clear about how to solve the Nicaraguan problem, but I was entirely certain that the solution lay in a change in the system, and I was fully conscious of the fact that only a truly leftist organization, only a revolutionary vanguard, in other words only a workers' party, could devote itself to the task of transforming society. In those days I thought I was going to find all this in the Socialist Youth.

At that time I was already convinced that it wasn't possible for "the rich to be concerned with the poor"—for purely objective reasons. That "concern" is against their own class interests. I also believed, and still do, that a great part of the solution to the Nicaraguan problem lay in being able to solve the peasant problem, the problem of land.

So I asked to be assigned to work in the countryside, and was sent to develop propaganda work in an area near the capital. Nevertheless, and in spite of having made some contacts, principally with young women, the work was not very productive. A lot of the problem was due to my political and ideological weakness.

Up to that time I hadn't engaged in much study that would have allowed me to develop my contacts politically, and more important, my attitude was a little paternalistic. I was terribly upset to see misery and I tried to teach those miserable people some job that would permit them to help each other . . . That was why I asked my mama to give me lessons in sewing—so I could teach the peasant women every weekend when I visited them. This will give you some idea of my inability to face the problem: I tried to solve the problem by *my* teaching them a job, instead of mobilizing not only the women but all the peasants to demand that the government pay attention to the problem. Besides, I think the way I became tied to that reality was a mistake; in practice there wasn't any tie, only an appearance, because I didn't recognize the total reality of the peasants I worked with. It turned out to be a little artificial.

In those days I was in my third year of the bachelor degree and had many acquaintances at the Institute, not only with my classmates but with students of other years, with professors who knew my anti-Somoza feelings and my inclinations toward the left, but even so I was politically removed from my environment, wasn't doing any work in the student movement, and besides, I don't think I ever recruited a single comrade in the Institute. Years later I found my study mates in the struggle—some fighting, others contributing . . .

" . . . something very direct against the system . . . "

In 1963 the Sandinist Front carried out its first "expropriation" in a Bank of America branch. The economic group in control of Bank of America activities is one of the most reactionary groups. It belongs to the conservative oligarchy, although at bottom it is closely tied up with the Somozas too; as is the case of Alfredo Pellas who, in the 1967 electoral campaign, gave more money to publicize Somoza than he gave to the candidate of his own party.

I was enthusiastic about this action because it dealt with something very direct against the sytem, but my attitude toward the event was nothing more than admiration. You have to understand this by bearing in mind my political and ideological level. I believed that in spite of the fact that there was no freedom in the country, no tradition of civic struggle, no respect for citizens' rights, there could in some way—without recourse to violence—be brought about the change in the system that was necessary. In other words, I had no clear idea of how to fight capitalism.

On March 20 of that year the FSLN occupied a radio station and broadcast a proclamation. Afterward, between July and October, the massacre of the Bocay guerrillas took place. All this made an impression on me . . .

In 1963 my trip to the Soviet Union to study at Patricio Lumumba University was arranged. In September I went to Moscow. Of course it was no easy matter. I was only 18 and I couldn't leave the country without the authorization of my parents. My mama gave me the authorization, but in the immigration office they didn't accept the document and so I had to take them a document signed by my papa.

I decided to put before my papa the need of his signing the paper, but of course he refused and the battle started. My mama didn't intervene directly; we considered it unwise since she was staying and my papa could make her responsible for my trip. It occurred to me to threaten my papa by telling him I'd join a guerrilla band if he didn't give me his permission. This worked. Apparently he was more informed than I, and he saw the armed movement as a real danger to the system.

In Moscow I became acquainted with other revolutionaries and with Marxist literature, and could study more methodically—or rather, methodically. During this time I met Nora Paiz, the Guatemalan guerrilla fighter who was assassinated in 1967 along with Otto Rene Castillo. Norita was very tiny, with a gentle character, very sweet like almost all Guatemalans . . . She leaned toward literature, probably hadn't written anything, but she enjoyed going to recitals. For reasons of security, I suppose, she never told me she had been directly connected with the guerrilla movement in her country, but she did tell me her family was leftist.

Together we visited the Komsomol school of painting to see a relative of hers who was a member of the Party or the Youth. I continued hearing about Norita through her in-laws who in 1967 wrote me of her death on March 19 of that year. I found out later the cruel way she had been killed. Out of respect for her, I baptized a short, 38 caliber revolver with the name Norita. It was small and effective like she was.

In Moscow I also met a Venezuelan girl who told me about the struggle they were supporting at that time. She told me about Livia Gouverneur and how she was assassinated by imperialism.

All these accounts, all the experiences of these and other comrades—many Cubans among them—together with the study of Marxist theory, made me understand the plans that comrade Oscar Turcios was making for me, and I realized it was necessary for me to return to my country and join the Sandinist Front. Oscar returned to Nicaragua in 1964, and I in 1965.

I married in the Soviet Union in 1964—an Ecuadorian comrade studying agronomy but who preferred literature—a poet. In 1965 my first child was born and I immediately went back to my country. Later, in 1967, I separated from this comrade.

That whole stage of my life, that is, from the time I began to serve in the Patriotic Youth in 1960 until 1965 when I returned to the country and joined the Sandinist Front, was one of the most valuable periods in my life. Though it's hard to say what period in a person's life is more or less valuable.

I believe that all the time lived "forging ahead," that is to say, maturing, correcting, and verifying ideas—is truly important for a person, and even more so for a militant. That's why I believe that this period was very valuable. I began to have a fighting spirit and

an organized and direct participation. I had a chance to bind
myself organically to the country's working class. I was able to
meet revolutionaries of other nations who influenced my life. I had
greater access to Marxist literature, which made me understand
the true role of the Party of the working class, and gave me a very
clear picture of my part in the struggle . . .

1965 - 1975

" . . . to participate more directly in the struggle."

When I returned to Nicaragua in December 1965, I told the Socialist Party of my decision to stop serving with them. I told them I thought it necessary to participate more directly in the struggle.

I looked for my comrade Oscar Turcios and let him know my decision. This was in 1966. Then he invited me to a meeting that was held on February 21 in commemoration of the assassination of General Sandino, and he told me he was going to inform the comrades responsible that I wanted to serve in the Organization. In that meeting comrade Turcios took the floor and quite clearly outlined the Organization's policies and made us see that a new electoral farce was coming and that before it came we must be on guard, that we mustn't let ourselves be carried away by the hopes the opposing bourgeoisie was trying to instil in us. On January 22, 1967, the correctness of this outline of the Organization's policies was confirmed.

More or less around that time it was decided that I would go and work with the Revolutionary Student Front (FER), a student organization controlled by the FSLN, and that later my membership in the Front would be decided. I worked in the Revolutionary Student Front with comrades Julio Buitrago, Humberto Ortega, Casimiro Sotelo and Michele Najlis. I matriculated in the School of Economics together with Oscar, because my work was going to be in that field.

In those days we worked on the publication of *The Student*, an FER periodical that has been coming out since 1965 and is still being published. To print this journal we had the collaboration of comrade Fernando Gordillow who was a member of the FSLN. We tried to get the journal out every two weeks, but I don't think we always succeeded. We had a lot of enthusiasm but very bad work methods; some of us were weighed down—or maybe it would be better to say I was weighed down—by petty bourgeois habits, and by craftsman-like work methods. We couldn't or weren't able to develop the work as far as we should have. I have to make clear to you that in addition, because of the needs of the Front, some of the comrades abandoned their work in the Revolutionary Student Front and went on to clandestine work. At the end of 1966 comrade Casimiro Sotelo had to leave the country, and this crippled the FER . . .

That year was a year of great activity. The Pancasan guerrilla movement was being prepared and everyone was doing something.

Oscar left for Guatemala with comrade Edmundo Perez and others, to learn from the experience of the Guatemalan guerrillas. They returned in November, almost at the end, it could even have been in October, I don't remember exactly . . . But it was on Oscar's return that I became more directly involved in the Organization. Before, and while I was working for the Revolutionary Student Front, I carried out some assignments for the Front, but I wasn't rightfully a militant. The work I was doing for the Front was in the field of propaganda or buying materials the guerrilla comrades needed. But my more direct, vital activity started from December 1966.

" . . . a hunger strike carried out by women . . ."

In 1966 there was a lot of activity by the people and the student movement in political matters. The Revolutionary Student Front (FER) decided to run a candidate in the student elections. We lost that election by seven votes. It hurt us. But we realized how much strength and prestige the Front had in the student body, and that we needed an organization now that we would be able to mobilize. The rival candidate was a member of the Christian Democratic Front and went to the elections in "holy" alliance with other sectors of the right, including Somoza supporters.

We also did some work in the Catholic University, the UCA,

which is the university of the bourgeoisie and the oligarchy. At that university Casimiro Sotelo was in his last year of law and was president of the Student Center there. Comrade Buitrago was also studying there, as were comrades David Tejada and Fernando Gordillo. These comrades were studying there because in order to study they had to work and only in Managua could they find jobs. Besides, they were studying law, and in Managua only the UCA had a law school.

Security knew about Casimiro's ability. The oligarchy, represented by the university authorities, couldn't forget the accusations Casimiro made in 1965 about the situation of the miners. So the authorities took advantage of any old thing and expelled him from the University. His expulsion gave rise to great indignation from the student body and the popular sectors who showed their repudiation of the UCA rector who, aside from being a priest, is a cousin of the Somozas.

In that year there was the liberal convention that named Somoza as candidate for the presidency, and the FER stated to the student movement the need to denounce this event with a hunger strike carried out by women in one of the University buildings. So we were in a hunger strike for about three or four days, the length of the convention. Students of the various departments and comrades who were representatives of worker organizations and leftist groups and a few representatives of the bourgeois opposition all took part in the strike.

". . . the nuns thought more like impresarios . . ."

In about 1966 or 1967, I can't remember exactly, my mama's family offered help so my sisters could go to the nuns' school in Managua. And when she took them to matriculate, the nuns told my mama that in order to accept the girls in the school I'd have to go out into the street or the girls would have to live with some relative.

The point was, they wouldn't accept girls living in the same house with me. My mama refused and finally the nuns thought more like impresarios . . . Just imagine—there were three girls, and with the high cost of those schools the amount the nuns could

lose if they stuck to their "principles" was great. So they
accepted my sisters.

When this happened my mama told me that when we had
recently moved to Managua, she wanted to enter my sisters in La
Asuncion school, run by nuns, and they weren't accepted because
they—my papa and mama—weren't married by the Church. When
she told me this, she said she was glad I had studied at the Institute because she wasn't humiliated by anybody.

"NO MORE SOMOZA."

There was a very important event: when the baseball league was
started, Tacho* attended. We knew he was going to go and we
decided to show our rejection of him there in the presence of all the
people who would be watching the game that day. We prepared a
great big piece of canvas and painted NO MORE SOMOZA on it,
and we mixed with the public congregated behind the stadium
where the teams starting the parade were. As it was the
inauguration, and Somoza was present, there were many people in
that place: children from the public schools who were taken there
willy-nilly to parade in front of the rostrum. We mingled with
these people—the musicians of the Guard band, and an occasional
Security agent. Of course those of us who were too impatient tried
not to be seen. Before the whole spectacle began, at a
pre-arranged signal, we jumped over the hedge and unrolled the
canvas.

At first the Security didn't know what was going on, and we
were able to run all around the stadium with the canvas unrolled.
The people shouted and cheered Sandino, the students, the
"twenty-third of July." They shouted "Death to Somoza!" It was
as if the sight of the canvas sign carried by the students had given
them courage to repudiate all the government people who were
there. I can imagine how enraged Somoza must have been . . .

It didn't take the Guard long to step into their role and come out
to massacre students. That day when the squad jumped down from
their vehicles to flog us, "the bird," a corporal known for his

* Somoza. Tacho is a diminutive of Anastasio.

cruelty, was among them. They pistol-whipped us, kicked us and succeeded in capturing some of our comrades. They arrested Casimiro because he was on the field trying to protect a woman comrade who was being pistol-whipped by Security.

Those of us who could escape did so, because the townspeople who sat in the bleachers protected us, tearing down the barrier and holding out their arms so we could get away. When we were able to scatter among the public, we changed the way we looked—as best we could—and went off immediately.

When no students were left on the field they went on with the inauguration. The people were restless but the public was not allowed to leave; they shut the gates. They thought that those who hadn't been arrested were still inside the stadium.

This act by Security cost seven or eight lives. When the game ended, and since Security hadn't been able to arrest any more of us, they kept the gates shut, all but one, and made the people go out through it. Security lined both sides of the exit line. That gate had a turnstile. The entire scene terrorized the people who, at the screams of the police, pushed the people in front who couldn't get out. Several persons lay dead against the turnstile, and others died trampled on or smothered. The next day they were all buried together, at one funeral. That was an enormous demonstration against the government, against Security.

" . . . I received the name of Conchita Alday."

In December 1966, at a meeting with the national administration of the Sandinist Front, I received the name of Conchita Alday. At that meeting, in which Oscar Turcios and other comrades of the administration participated, it was explained to me who Conchita Alday was. I was made to see that the name of Conchita Alday must be borne with dignity, that I had to respect her, had to deserve the honour of bearing the name of this comrade.

Conchita Alday was the comrade of General Francisco Sequera, known by the name of General "Cabulla." General "Cabulla" was a man of the common people who in 1926 fought the invading Yankees. General "Cabulla" was in charge of the western zone; that was his field of action. He took charge of harassing the railway

line by which the Yankee marines who disembarked at the port of
Corinto reached the capital city. General "Cabulla" took part in
the battle of Chinandega, one of the bloodiest battles of the time.
The city of Chinandega was bombed for several hours by the
Yankee planes.

His comrade, Conchita Alday, took part with him as a
combatant. General "Cabulla," in spite of being a man of the
people didn't have the capability that General Sandino was
shown to have. He stayed in the Viejo zone, in the department of
Chinandega. And there he was surprised by the Yankee army. He
was surprised in a house, together with his comrade. At that time
Conchita was in an advanced state of pregnancy, and the *gringo*
soldiers slit open her belly with their bayonets to take out the fetus
while she was still alive, and later they quartered her completely.

It was her name that in 1966 the national administration of the
Sandinist Front decided I should have, and it was at that meeting it
was given to me. I worked for a year with her name, that is, until
Security found out that Conchita Alday was me, and on November
19, 1967 I was arrested after comrade Casimiro Sotelo had been
assassinated. The oldest comrades in the organization still call me
Conchita . . .

Around that time Casimiro left the country and comrade
Buitrago and I remained in the city. Julio was a member of the
National Administration and I worked with him on supply
problems. The electoral campaign was coming to an end and the
FSLN made public a document explaining our position and the
decision to undertake armed struggle.

". . . that brutalizes women . . ."

On January 20, 1967, there was an "expropriation" in which
comrade Francisco Moreno took part. Frank, as we used to call
him, was a very young comrade whom I knew when he was a child.
His father was a doctor and for a time, when Frank was four years
old or less, they lived in Matagalpa across from my house.

There's something about Frank I've always remembered. He
was always saying that "domestic service brutalizes" . . . Those
may not have been his exact words, but you get the idea. Once he

referred to this seriously and said to me: "Refuse to do domestic work in security houses; that brutalizes women . . ."

Frank was eighteen, in high school, and had been working for the Organization for a long time. Once he was ordered to do some work in Matagalpa. At that time the Organization was already arranging some means of support for the comrades who were working "professionally" for the Front. Yet Frank never took a *cinco* for himself.

I had given him a contact for when he might need something , a girl friend of mine since childhood days, a girl with money . . . She told me she was impressed to see Frank arrive with his worn-out shoes and poorly clothed. In spite of the money, he managed. At another time a co-worker told me he had given him money to buy clothes and shoes, and Frank used the money to buy paper to print some flyers.

"Somoza being an animal . . ."

On January 22 the people demonstrated against the regime, the last demonstration permitted before the elections and probably the last till another electoral farce when the opposition bourgeoisie engage in political demagogy.

At this demonstration they sang songs against the Somozas and popular songs about Sandino. A stanza from one of them goes:

> Tacho Somoza killed
> to come to power
> Tacho Somoza killed
> to come to power
> First he had to murder
> first he had to murder
> first he had to murder
> Augusto Cesar Sandino.
> Somoza being an animal
> his picture's on a bill
> Somoza being an animal
> his picture's on a bill
> he had to kill Sandino first

    to climb that hill
    to climb that hill
    to climb that hill.

This was sung to a Mexican tune.

Nicaraguan popular music is very much tied up with Mexican music. Since Sandino days, the "Adelita" melody has been used for the words of the revolutionary songs sung in the encampments.

The January 22 demonstration was broken up and the people who were protesting unarmed were massacred. All day long and during the days that followed we could hear shots and see guards pistol-whipping the people who hadn't been able to get to their homes.

Security makes use of the Nicaraguan Red Cross, puts their agents into the ambulances, and in this way they get into the midst of all the people who don't suspect that in the ambulances— supposedly meant to take away the dead and wounded—come the Security agents who climb out firing at the people.

The election campaign was a very bloody one and during registration they assassinated Silvio Parodi, an opponent of the regime who was serving in the Conservative Party. Silvio was killed by Somoza's Guard near one of the registration tables. Afterwards Aguero contracted with the Guard to have one of his most loyal followers killed.

" . . . in the 'democracies' . . ."

On January 23 they arrested me in my house. Captain Nicolas Valle Salinas arrested me—the same one who on July 23, 1960 commanded the squad that pistol-whipped me. Security knew I had nothing to do with the events of the twenty-second, but they arrested me for "national security" reasons and I was detained for thirteen days.

There were a lot of prisoners, townspeople of the petty bourgeoisie and bourgeois people who went out under amnesty on the eve of the elections—because of the idea that in the "democracies," elections are held in a climate of peace and harmony.

I spent my thirteen days of detention in a migration prison called the "Shelter." They didn't torture me physically since they didn't know about my activity with the Front. They didn't know I was Conchita Alday. But in Security there was a guy who busied himself by coming to my cell at any odd moment, and he started telling me they were going to bring my son, who was a year and four months old then, to see if he could stand one day in their hands. This fellow was Lieutenant Torres, known as "Goiter Torres."

The elections were held and Somoza "won." You can see the correctness of the FSLN's plans, but the opposition didn't gain any experience like the other parties of the bourgeoisie, and years later when the other elections were approaching, the Conservative Party, and Aguero himself, made a pact with Somoza.

Meanwhile, the guerrillas were trying to increase, to recruit from the peasantry. Acts of "expropriation" were being planned in the city for the purpose of getting money and making propaganda.

" . . . what he had to do was return the blows . . . "

On August 5, 1967, an act of "expropriation" was carried out in the "La Perfecta" dairy. Unfortunately things didn't turn out as well as was expected. The Security forces showed up before the comrades could escape, and they were surrounded. Comrade Selim Schible was killed in the fight and comrades Jacinto Suarez and Humberto Catum were taken prisoner; the latter got out later.

Selim was a comrade who joined the revolutionary movement when very young. He was barely twenty-four when he died. He had been arrested many times, I believe some thirteen or fourteen times. He was tortured by Gonzalo Lecayo, a Security cop who was put to death by the FSLN the same year. Selim used to say that when a person has been taken prisoner, what he had to do was return the blows the agents gave him, so they'd become so furious they'd knock him out. "That's how you'd be sure not to talk," he used to say. He was very brave. In the incident I'm telling you about, when he was tortured by Gonzalo Lacayo, he attacked that pig, and if I'm not mistaken he broke one of his ribs or fractured his skull. Of course Selim was killed in the most inhumane way.

I told you that Selim was jailed very often. In 1961 or 1962 he was arrested in Guatemala as he was trying to get to Cuba. So Selim said he was a *gusano** who had to get into Cuba secretly; the Guatemalan Security took him to prison to some *gusanos* belonging to "Alfa-66" so they'd recognize him and prove it wasn't true. Those *gusanos* tortured Selim and the other comrades.

" . . . was captured alive; they tortured him to death . . ."

On August 28, news came that thirteen comrades had been killed in Pancasan. It was a very hard blow. Valuable comrades fell, with years of struggle under their belts, with long experience. Comrades with great human qualities, like Rigoberto Cruz, Carlos Reyna, Francisco Moreno, Fausto Garcia, Silvio Mayorga, Oscar Danilo Rosales, Otto Casco, Fermin Diaz, Ernesto Fernandez, Felipe Gaitan and Carlos Tinoco.

Oscar Danilo Rosales was a young doctor, a graduate of the University, who had been participating since his students years in the struggle of the Nicaraguan people. Oscar took part in the 1962 meeting to organize the FER. When the guerrillas were preparing he had already graduated and had a professorship in the University. He also had recently married. When he joined the guerrillas he sent a letter to the University regents telling them of his decision and criticizing the attitude of that body. Oscar was captured alive; they tortured him to death.

In the camp and the mountains there was a great deal of terror, the Guard killing entire families. That was when we found out about the Security's concentration camps in all the mountains of the north and in other places. In one of the roundups they captured one of my first cousins who was involved with the guerrillas, comrade Oscar Armando Flores. They killed him. They killed this comrade terribly. They skinned him with a "Gillette" or some such thing, lifted all his skin with a "Gillette" . . . and then put salt or vinegar, I don't remember . . . He was left there till he died.

---

* A "worm," a Cuban counter-revolutionary.

They didn't even bury him; I understand he was thrown off a cliff.

I remember Silvio Mayorga from those days. This comrade was very sensitive. When he was detailed for the mountains, he once sent me a little note in which he wrote that what affected him most in his mountain work was that where he was there was no farmhouse where sick children could get well. For it seemed that all the peasant children in the country were sick—with diarrhea, covered with rashes . . . He asked me for medicine for the children.

At Christmas he sent me another note asking me to somehow get some caramels or toys, because the children had never had a toy—not even one sweet of the cheapest kind. Those children live a totally marginal existence, never enjoying any of the satisfactions enjoyed by a city child, or even a country child if its parents happen to be plantation owners. They are children who don't even know Christmas exists.

In 1967 when the Pancasan guerrilla bands were being formed, I had a chance to meet a comrade from a peasant background but who came from a city, also in the north. This comrade was or had been tubercular. That's why we were giving him some special vitamins. From his daily dose he would hold aside one vitamin tablet and put it in a little bottle apart.

I asked him what he wanted those for, and he said he had to keep them and would tell me why on another occasion. After August 1967 when the deaths of the Pancasan comrades occurred, I didn't see this comrade for a long time, not till 1968—almost a year after the guerrilla fighting. Later he told me that the vitamins he had put away were for his mama who was sick. And just when he had the chance to go home or get those vitamins to his home his mother died. This comrade told me he had felt very bad because at the exact moment when he could have had the vitamins reach his mama, they were no longer of any use.

Edmundo Perez succeeded in escaping from Pancasan with his life.

"She's a mother of communists . . ."

In November 1967, November 4, Security discovered a hideout and captured alive comrades Casimiro Sotelo, Roberto Amaya,

Hugo Medina and Edmundo Perez, the one who escaped the
Pancasan massacre. When the squad entered the house there was
a volley of gunfire, but the comrades were captured. In the
shooting comrade Edmundo Perez suffered a leg wound.

Hours later Security reported that the comrades had been killed
in the gunfire. The family of one of them told me that the body was
full of dirt and had to be washed, and was still bleeding. The death
had apparently taken place minutes before the body was handed
over to the family.

Casimiro Sotelo's body showed a bayonet wound at the height of
the jugular vein. Roberto Amaya's body had cigarette burns all
over it. The bodies of comrade Sotelo and the other comrades had
the same number of bullet holes as the Security police officer
Gonzalo Lecayo who had been executed in that year. The bodies
were handed over on condition they be buried immediately, but
the townspeople got wind of when the burial was to take place and
there were popular demonstrations opposing the regime and the
system.

Gladys Baez was captured along with those other comrades.

The squad that went to this fight was commanded by Alesio
Gutierrez, a lieutenant at the time. He was promoted because of his
"heroism." The truth is that he was promoted in compensation for
making himself responsible for the slaughter committed by
Security. Alesio is a servile fellow who started his criminal career
very young. He started as orderly to General Gustavo Montiel,
commanding officer of the Office of National Security, many years
ago. For a time he worked collecting "whores' dollars," as they
call the *mordida* (percentage or tip) the prostitutes are forced to
give the authorities. Later, that same Alesio was head warden of
Aviation Prison where he was equally cruel to both the political
and common prisoners. At present he's commander of Jinotega
and is distinguished there for his pitiless treatment of the peasant
population. Alesio comes from a humble and honourable family.

After these happenings I was arrested for the second time, on
November 19. The guards came to the house on the pretext of
looking for a supposedly stolen vehicle, and said it had been seen
near my house. Since they couldn't find me, they took my mama.
They held her as a hostage and would let her go only on the
condition that I surrender. I waited because I knew they couldn't

hold her for long. She was set free eight or nine days later, but not without going through a bad time.

She was treated very badly. She told me there were a great number of people, for example a lady who had a little store near a house where the comrades used to go, a place where food was sold—grain, rather, but on a small scale; a very small, tiny little store. This lady's children would take food to her, and my mama told me that then the guards came and said: "Look at the difference: you can see this lady's a good Christian who's trained her children well and they bring her food and look out for her! That other old woman," referring to my mama, "you can see she gave birth to a lot of snakes. She's a mother of Communists and that's why they don't bring her any food, and nobody comes to ask her about her. There she is, calm as . . ."

They treated her very badly; she said that one of the guards even tried to handle her. They set her free in eight or nine days. I was hiding in my own house, but they found me anyway. On the nineteenth they realized where I was and arrested me. They sentenced me to six months in jail for violating the Political Constitution.

Comrade Gladys Baez was in prison at the time. She had been very badly treated, her underpants were all torn because they undressed her and her pants were torn to bits. She was punished by being made to prop herself against a wall by the tips of her thumbs and her toes.

A very young comrade was also a prisoner: Yolanda Nunez. She was pregnant. They had taken her with her comrade. They stripped her and put her in humiliating positions and beat her in front of her companion to make him talk. Elba Campos was also being held there; she too was pregnant but was about seven or eight months along. She had an enormous belly . . . She was being held because she was the girl friend of a militant and they assumed she was collaborating or had something to do with the Front. Also, about eight other comrades were being held, three of whom had been raped. In the case of one of those raped comrades, we were able to find out that one of her rapists was a Security agent named "Alvarenga"; we even learned that Somoza himself had taken part in these rapes.

The situation for us—that is, for Gladys and me—was very bad.

The two pregnant comrades were isolated, put into solitary, not brought food and not permitted to receive any. Yolanda had suffered so many blows that we were afraid she might lose the baby, but luckily she had no problem. We had to pull strings in order to get some food for them. On that occasion, thanks to the solidarity of the other regular prisoners, we were able to at least assure them of food once.

The food question . . . prison meals in Nicaragua are very bad. We called the food they gave us *chupeta* (pacifier), a poorly-put-together corn tortilla with a very bad taste and very small. The size of a little plate, the kind used for dessert. Once we were able to count thirty-eight grains of rice and fourteen beans. That's a prison ration. Especially for pregnant women, this was no meal. And we were given it only three times a day, nothing else, and always the same thing. We were able to get a loan, to buy some milk.

After that we were put under house arrest, that is Gladys, Elba and I. But Yolanda, the youngest, wasn't able to obtain her freedom. In spite of her urging, the comrade had to stay in prison for a lot longer. She succeeded in being released almost when she was about to give birth. A little before she had the baby, she too was put under house arrest. That was at the end of 1967.

House arrest: I don't know if it's the same in all countries. You must have a guarantor, a person offering to guarantee to answer for you, and then you have to stay inside that house, the house of the guarantor. You can't leave, can't go out.

" . . . the Internationale."

In my life in the Organization and among the women comrades, I had the chance to get to know Gladys Baez better. She was a valued comrade. She was my age. She comes from a small agricultural town too. She was the only daughter of a woman of the people, a woman who devoted her whole life to washing and ironing. Gladys married very young and had two children from that marriage. She worked to help support her family. At her job she joined other workers—first in union work and then in the Organization. She was a comrade who never had the opportunity to study much, to go

Gladys Baez, comrade and friend.

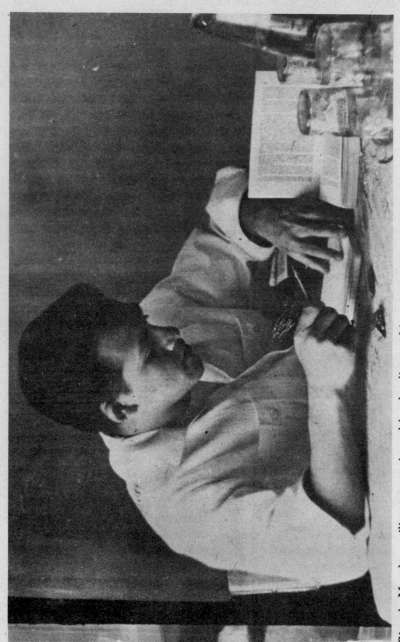

Ricardo Morales, militant assassinated by the dictatorship

to school. She developed basically through her militancy and her reading. Yet she was very able.

Once she told me she had to face some very difficult situations in her life. First, her husband loved to drink and he abandoned her with two little ones. She had to work, and to top it off she plunged into union affairs and went to the meetings and talked about socialism and the Cuban Revolution.

Once, because of her activities, the priest in her town excommunicated her. The consequences of this was that in the stores they wouldn't even sell her any food, much less extend credit. She told me her family wouldn't even visit her or give her any help because she'd been excommunicated. At one point she thought she was going to starve because she couldn't buy tortillas or corn meal or anything at all. No store would even sell her salt.

Her union comrades said she should move out of the town but she refused. She refused to leave the town and said she'd survive, that she was going to break the isolation imposed by the priest. With the help of some comrades she obtained food and continued working in the union, kept on going to the meetings till, little by little—this over many years and with a lot of struggle and a great deal of explaining to people—she reestablished her relationships and was able to make the people practically lift the "moral" disgrace that was weighing her down. She has still remained firm after all these years. Her mother is sick now, practically paralysed. For Gladys the situation is difficult because she has to attend to her children.

Gladys is the comrade responsible for the work done in the Patriotic Alliance of Nicaraguan Women. When the Alliance was organized there were no materials for communiques, for issuing bulletins, and it was amazing to see how Gladys got things from nowhere. She taught herself to use a typewriter, learned to draw, even wrote revolutionary songs and poems.

She is a woman with unimaginable resources. She never leaves a job unfinished for lack of means or because there's no one to write a communique. She's really a comrade who can lift the spirits of any militant. It's incredible to see how she makes really extraordinary efforts and accomplishes jobs, almost without preparation or resources. She has never refused to do a job because she didn't have the ability or wasn't given enough to work with.

Gladys is such an extraordinary person that she really makes you stop and think when some small difficulty keeps you from doing a job or makes you lose heart. I've never seen her sad. In spite of all her family problems, all she's suffered, she's a comrade who keeps her spirits up.

When we were together in prison, she organized cultural sessions with the regular prisoners. And she conducted study circles without any study materials. She used the *Internationale*. She would recite a stanza of the anthem and then we'd begin to talk about what each one of us knew about each moment, about each situation the *Internationale* touches. It was really admirable, also, to see how she was constantly interested in the problems of the others, while she had many of her own. Once her mother wrote her that her two children couldn't go to school because they had no shoes. Her answer was that they should be sent barefooted, and if they weren't welcome without shoes then they should be left at home. Yet even while her mother was telling her about her own children's problem, she was concerned about the children of the other comrades, and it was then that she organized a little party to celebrate the birthday of my son.

This gives you an idea of the solidarity and human qualities of this comrade; even though her own children didn't have the clothes or shoes to go to school with, and had no pencils or notebooks, she was trying to figure out how to celebrate the birthday of a child of a comrade in prison.

She worried, for example, about how the children of the dead comrades, the children of the imprisoned comrades, could have a little party and some presents for Christmas. She herself sometimes even made dolls and was constantly concerned with the children of others, and happily so. She never let the condition of her own children make her bitter. Maybe her children didn't have any presents for Christmas, and she was making dolls for the children of other comrades . . .

"He told how he had seen his brother die . . ."

In 1968, the first months of 1968, I think it was March or April, they arrested David Tejada. He was beaten to death by Oscar Morales, known as "Moralito." At the time David was captured and killed—it was during Holy Week—this "Moralito" went around with his hand bruised. Drunk on a beach one day, he told people he had injured it beating a prisoner. This aroused suspicion about David's situation. Pressure was applied and David was asked to be brought before the judge.

That's how they found out David was dead. The Guard convened a court to investigate the cause of death. David had been arrested with his brother Rene. So Rene was taken to the court and he testified how "Moralito" had killed David. Rene had also been beaten and he related how David had had an eye totally gouged out and been completely disemboweled from blows on all sides. He was lashed with wire by "Moralito" himself. He told how he had seen his brother die without even being able to get near him because he too was being beaten. After this the Guard was obliged to hand over Rene right then and there.

Popular demonstrations were held every day. The University Student Union had a permanent funeral vigil demanding to have the body handed over. We knew because of the statements of some guards, that the cadaver had been tossed into the crater of the Santiago volcano. There were demonstrations—demonstrations by the people—all the way to the volcano itself. Many townspeople offered to rescue the body, but the crater is very big. Some people even arrived with special equipment and climbed down to a certain point, but they never found the body. Since then the Santiago volcano has been popularly known as Tejada volcano.

All this time demonstrations were taking place in the cities, as many in the capital as in other departments. And the townspeople were constantly inside the University Club at the permanent funeral vigil. Market women came, and working women, carrying floral offerings, and they kept watch there all night long—people who worked all day . . .

" . . . I went into hiding."

It was then that they announced the arrival of US President
Lyndon Johnson. It was planned for July 8, 1968. On the thirtieth
of May that year the Revolutionary Student Front carried out an
action—May 30 is Mothers' Day in Nicaragua—an action
commemorating the mothers of the Sandinist Front martyrs.

The bourgeois opposition press that has always been
characterized by its subtle denunciations of the actions of the
Sandinist Front militants, was always printing: "Doris Tijerino was
at a meeting and she took the floor . . ." It wasn't interested in
what I said. Sometimes it wasn't even true that I'd been there. But
since I had the house for a jail, I was constantly being called by the
judge and threatened with being taken prisoner again.

The judge had called me in a few days before Johnson arrived,
and had said he couldn't wait for the police any more, that
undoubtedly I was going to be arrested. We saw the need of my
hiding during the time of Johnson's visit. The Revolutionary
Student Front had also organized a lot of activities and
demonstrations repudiating and protesting Johnson's visit to the
country. Traffic was stopped. Groups of students and militants
from the Front in small squads stopped the traffic and climbed
onto the city buses . . . They passed out leaflets or took the floor
and held spur-of-the-moment meetings inside vehicles.

It was a question of coming to where Johnson would be lodged.
Demonstrations denouncing Johnson's visit went on all along the
route taken by him and his party. Many were arrested. Mainly
students. Then Security made use of this to repress the leaders of
the Front who were at the University. They came to get me, but
they couldn't find me. I had gone into hiding.

In hiding it was my job to print leaflets and communiques; they
put me in charge of propaganda—the technical part of it, the
mimeographing of leaflets edited by the Organization for study in
the cells and the flyers to be distributed in the peoples' sectors.

" . . . where men and women work together, women are very seldom executives . . ."

The cell I worked in was in charge of planning and providing orientation to the women's organization: the Patriotic Alliance of Nicaraguan Women. This wasn't a clandestine organization and we weren't members of it, but our jobs were to orient the work the legal comrades were to carry out. This organization was composed of women of popular extraction, proletarians, some students—mostly working women. Women of the people. It stated that its main objective was to overcome women's inferiority and to struggle for better working conditions for women—equality in matters of wages, for social security for domestic workers, especially the right to vacations and one day a week off, and for better treatment for all women workers.

Most working women are given very hard jobs, mainly in textile mills and match factories. There are a great number of women in match factories. The work is very poorly paid and very painstaking because a match is a tiny thing and the pay is very little for packing an enormous quantity of little match sticks that have to be counted by hand. The working conditions are very bad and so is the pay. The jobs are filled mostly by women.

Part of our struggle was to get working women unionized. Women had very little participation in the country's union life as there were very few unionized women and where they were union members their participation was minimal. They didn't lead a very active life—it's evident in unions where there are men only a few women achieve executive positions. Most of the union heads are men. For example, in the Aceitera Corona (Crown Oil Processing Plant) where men and women work together, women are very seldom executives, and aren't seen very often in the meetings themselves. Women are union heads only for jobs like nursing which employ only women.

This isn't the case among teachers, for example. Here women do take a great part, first because of their number, and also because they've had to have a greater preparation. I think there are more women than men teachers and women carry more weight than men in the field of education. It's a profession that's been practiced almost solely by women for a long time . . .

The women's organization's stated objective was to develop
women's participation, both by making women cónscious of their
duty to take part in union life and by making the men permit
women to participate.

The Front would orient the work—orient it politically. As for its
practical direction, the responsibility was placed on the legal
comrades—on those from the Front and on others who weren't
members. But the principal objective was to make proletarian
women and women of the people participate.

Some work was organized toward this end, some meetings and
assemblies were held. It seemed that all was going quite well.
Then July 15 arrived . . .

*"The policy of the Front was not aimed at repressing the guard,
the common guard . . ."*

Meanwhile, other activities were being carried out—"expropriations." There was an "expropriation" at another branch of the
Bank of America, the Buenos Aires branch, on September 20,
1968. The "expropriations" being carried out by the Front have
armed propaganda and recovery of the people's money as
objectives. This September 20 action took place days after Samuel
Genie, chief of the Office of Security, announced ín a press
conference that the Sandinist Front had been exterminated.

One week later the action was carried out, and Security never
"kicked the ball", as we used to say. It was totally disconcerted,
and didn't know what people had taken part in the action.

It was a very good action militarily, carried out in short order,
and didn't give the people a chance to see a single face. A guard
died in that action. The comrade in charge of watching outside the
building thought that the guard on duty had shot a comrade. They
hadn't seen him but undoubtedly he was going to shoot one of
them and he might have caused the death of all of them. The
comrade felt obliged to shoot this guard and kill him.

This guard was of peasant origin. The policy of the Front was
not aimed at repressing the guard, the common guard, because
they too are part of the people, and we're conscious of the fact that
these guards see themselves as pushed by the situation of the

country itself, because of lack of work, lack of opportunity, and inability to study and move ahead. Despite our principle of not firing at guards simply to kill them, the comrade felt obligated to shoot that guard. This was in September.

"They had been checking on Ricardo for a long time . . . "

Later, my comrade professor Ricardo Morales was taken prisoner in the street on December 11 or 12. This comrade was a member of the National Leadership and had been allied with the Front for many years, since he'd been studying in Mexico where he graduated with a degree in teaching methods. He was very ideologically advanced and possessed great political ability. When he came back to the country, he became a professor at the University while at the same time working with the Organization. At a certain stage in the development of his work with the FSLN, he felt obliged to quit the University and devote himself completely to the struggle.

They had been checking on Ricardo for a long time but they hadn't found a reason to arrest him until they found out that he had taken some part in the September 20 attack. He was arrested after a car chase through the city. They made him crash into a wall. He was taken out of his car nearly unconscious. They tortured him.

As for us, the day before we had had to abandon a house in a neighbourhood which the Security agents inspected with a fine-tooth comb, house by house. We realized what was happening and that we had to leave. The Guard actually did come, and though we were able to rescue some of the things in the house we couldn't rescue them all. It was daytime and thus impossible to go out with very big things like the mimeograph machine I was working with, and typewriters . . . The Guard found our equipment and succeeded in arresting a family that was serving as a cover in the house.

We gave orders for everyone to leave; it was daytime and each person went off on his own. But that family remained, and because they did Security was able to find out the identity of the people living in the house, my comrade and me among them. So the next day he was arrested.

*". . . and they always talked to me about the Front and watched
my face to see what expression I'd show."*

In those days I had an experience . . . I was practically without
any contacts because, well, in the first place I had left the house
and only my comrade knew where I was. He was arrested the next
day and from then I was left totally isolated from the rest of the
Organization. Through an emergency contact I was connected with
my comrades again. I moved to another place where it had been
decided I should go.

When I arrived another problem awaited me: the family was
unexpectedly visited by a relative, and so I couldn't stay in that
house. The lady of the house gave me the address of a
working-class woman in one of the most miserable neighbourhoods. I had to arrive at night without the knowledge of the
comrade living there: she couldn't be sure of who I was. I came to
the house and told her that I came from a town and was to have
been taken in by another lady who was a friend of hers. But that I
had had problems and couldn't stay there as her house was very
full. In other words, I told a really very weak story, but the woman
accepted me.

She was very poor, extremely poor. She didn't have a steady job
and lived by peddling. She'd sell vegetables one day, fruit
another, used clothes and old shoes another. And she had a lot of
children, seven or eight. The oldest was about twelve.

They had a very small house with only one room. There was no
drinking water. As these houses are situated near the lake, they
sink a shallow well and the water filtering in from the lake is what
they drink. That water is very dirty because all the polluted water
from the city drains into Managua Lake. As a result the water has
a layer of greenish scum on top.

The mother and her companion, who wasn't the father of her
children, of most of them, would go out to work very early. The
children would stay alone and were the responsibility of the oldest
girl, who was twelve. A smaller girl of nine had to do the cooking
because the twelve-year-old had to go out too—from house to
house to find someone who might need her services as a laundress.
She'd do a little washing and with what she earned she bought a
few beans, the only thing they ate all day . . .

There was no kitchen but they made a *tenamaste*—three big stones, with firewood in the middle and on top the casserole to cook in. Every time one of the little ones was hungry, she was served a few spoonfuls of what was in the pot, it was put in the child's hand or on a leaf. Of course the children had diarrhea all the time. The house smelled of excrement. It was horrible.

There was a boy of two who hadn't been bathed in who knows how long . . . probably not since he was born. His whole body was covered with pimples. His little ear was surrounded by pimples and it seemed as if he wasn't going to be able to hear.

The day I arrived I said I was going to bathe him and . . . His sister, the oldest girl, told me she had taken him to the hospital where the poor are attended to but they hadn't paid him any attention because they ask two dollars from the very poor people who go there to receive care. They didn't have the two dollars that gave them the right to a consultation at the general hospital.

They didn't have a toilet either, much less a bathroom. They had to attend to the calls of nature at the side of the house or squat behind a bush. The little nine-year-old girl in charge of the cooking had something the matter with one eye, like a tumor. The eye was closed and useless . . .

They were very intelligent children. I started studying with them while I was there; they had a great facility for learning mathematics. They even succeeded in spelling a few words. They didn't go to school. And that was in the capital—behind the pasteurization plant called "La Salud" (health), a milk processing plant owned by the Somoza family.

So those people had me there never asking me who I was or where I was going. They must have really thought I was a very suspicious person because I never went out during the day and I asked them not to tell the neighbours I was there, that if somebody saw me they should tell them I was a relative of theirs, from another town.

For me it was a very valuable experience because it taught me how they lived right there in the capital. I became aware of the solidarity of those people who must have known without any doubt that I was from the Front. When they returned at night they gave me news, and they always talked to me about the Front and watched my face to see what expression I'd show.

I was there for nine or ten days until I was moved by my comrades through an emergency contact.

"Housing for *my brother . . ."*

While I was in that house, Nicaragua was visited by a fellow who was in some way connected with housing. This man talked about the housing problem being resolved by the government, and also about the INVI quarters that are very bad developments, but undoubtedly they're palaces compared with that place.

INVI is the National Institute of Housing; it's an organization, an autonomous entity of the government. So this guy was saying that the INVI was solving the housing problem and was building houses for anyone who could give a high down payment and pay by the month. But it wasn't solving the problem of housing for the people. At that time I wrote a letter to the newspaper *La Prensa* signed with my name, inviting that man to visit those places. The letter described how those people lived and criticized a priest who had devoted his time to raising money for a project, a program called "Housing of my brother."

This priest planned to build a series of houses for very poor people, and he spent years on that project and built some very bad houses. He received aid from every known charitable organization, public and private. It was a swindle. The townspeople called "Housing of my brother" "Housing *for* my brother" because this priest had a brother and so they connected the program with *his* brother.

In the end the letter was used only for an article on the editorial page of *La Prensa* where they only printed fragments, and left out all that touched on the bourgeois sectors of opposition that participated in the construction along with the government. So they totally lessened the value of the criticism, because all they printed were a few sentences from the letter . . .

All that time I was working in the Patriotic Alliance of Women and that's why I was placed in a house in a place called *Delicias del Volga* near the Alliance. Comrade Julio Buitrago lived in that house where on July 15th the Guard squad came, and in the fighting comrade Buitrago was killed and I was arrested.

" . . . a scandal had occurred in the government . . . "

But some months before this, a scandal had occurred in the government. It was the rape of a student by Somoza's private secretary, Professor Jose Maria Zelaya. This fellow had organized the Liberal Students' Front. Their initials said quickly are confusing: FEL and FER—you can't distinguish them. You have to pronounce them very clearly to distinguish the name of the FEL.

It was the organization by means of which the government tried to penetrate the University and carry out some political activity. The Somozas have never been able to control the student movement. The student movement in Nicaragua has always been controlled by the opposition; the Nicaraguan students have a long tradition of struggle that deserves the respect of all the popular sectors, and the workers' movement recognizes the student movement as a revolutionary force in the country. This is a very special question in Nicaragua.

I'm not putting too much value on the role of the student movement, for it really does understand that the motive force behind the revolution has to be the working class. The students have won participation in the revolutionary struggle of the Nicaraguan people by their rebelliousness. The Nicaraguan students have been characterized by their stand against the Somozas and by their anti-imperialism.

This tradition of struggle, this anti-Somoza position and straight line policy held by the student movement in the face of the dictatorship, is worthy of recognition as a revolutionary student body. And that's why the worker has always turned to the student. And students have always involved themselves in the workers' struggle.

At no time has the student movement in Nicaragua been a movement that gives in. Even in the years when it was controlled by the social Christians who are a very vacillating force, the foundations of the student movement pressured and obligated these people to join the popular struggles, to state their policy as always being in favour of the workers' movement.

So, wanting to penetrate the University, the Liberal Party of Somoza organized the FEL which was made up mainly of students—many young people who were government employees.

It has never had a base at the National University, and has never acted in its own name. The statutes of the National Union of Students forbid membership for any student affilliated with the Liberal Party of Somoza. Even the University Center has the prerogative of demanding the expulsion of students who reveal themselves as partisans of Somoza or are proved to be such.

Those people worked inside the University, above all as spies. The FEL held a meeting back then, and professor Zelaya took this boy—Anastasio Real. He was employed by the government, a very young boy, and after the meeting the professor invited him to the Presidency. There he raped him. He raped him on his desk. Comrade Real denounced the act and of course he received the support and protection of the student movement. He had to stay for many days in the University Club and in the University Center offices, for protection.

On July 15, when the Guard raided our house, besides the papers of the Patriotic Alliance of Women they found other papers—a photo copy of this boy's statements. Then the Guard tried to make people believe that this boy had slandered professor Zelaya by express orders from the Front. As this was not true—we had the documents proving that it was a scandalous act by a member of the government—we, through the FER, steered the student movement to support this boy.

" . . . before dying, cried 'Long live Sandino!' "

On July 15 I'd been working on these statements, and on the desk, beside the typewriter, had those papers and others of the Patriotic Alliance. Because it was about three in the afternoon, I went down to the ground floor—the house had two storeys—to talk over something with comrade Buitrago.

While we were sitting there—he had his back to a window and I was facing it—I saw someone go by, running very quickly, and immediately heard a butt of a gun give a short knock on the door. Comrade Buitrago ran to the back of the house—he was only carrying regulation arms, I think a nine millimeter pistol or a forty-five. I had a thirty-eight revolver, my *Norita*.

There was a woman comrade in the house with us—since

comrade Buitrago and I were very suspect, very *hot*, we couldn't go out in the daytime—who was in charge of doing the shopping, and she was leading a perfectly legal life. She was the wife of one of our comrades who was later killed. She lived there with her two children. At that moment the older child wasn't at home; he had been sent off to school and there was only the little one, about three years old. When we ran to the back of the house to get to the second floor, the little girl came running inside. Then comrade Buitrago ordered me to return and take the child out. Meanwhile, he went upstairs to get an M-3 he had on the top floor.

I had to go and get the child because the Guard were already inside the house and shooting. I was able to take the child out to the courtyard and give her to her mother so she could leave with her little daughter. I told her not to come near the house. Then I returned.

I found Julio on the stairs shot from behind. He was wounded, and since the Guard were shooting, he had had to drop where he was, and so was lying on the stairs. Some Security agents came in, there were shots and as a result the Security agent acting as the head man was shot. When the Guard saw their man wounded, they ran out and left him inside. He was only wounded, but the guy didn't fall down right away. He kept on walking, stumbling along, succeeded in grabbing me, and wouldn't let me go.

At that moment Buitrago was able to climb to the second floor. When they came in to get the man, I still hadn't been able to work myself free, and they caught me. They left me sitting in front of the house all the time the fighting lasted. That fellow died later. The fighting lasted for about two and a half hours and it was an extraordinary thing. The Guard was as if out of control; they looked like when you kick an anthill and the ants run every which way. They were screaming, jumping around, driving a half track.

Afterward I realized that the woman comrade and her little girl hadn't been able to escape, but succeeded in staying out of range of the gunfire. The Guard was holding them.

After an hour and a half of fighting, or maybe less, they put me into a Security car and left its radio on. I found out that one of the small airplanes firing at the house was being piloted by a fellow named Rivas. They never said his first name but I heard them say Rivas.

I heard them giving orders to Security to move to another part of the city where they'd find other comrades. Besides, the Guard thought there were other people in the house because they couldn't conceive of one man holding off some three or four hundred guards for two and a half hours. They entered the house after the comrade died. After two and a half hours of fighting.

Julio, before dying, cried "Long live Sandino!" and sang a few stanzas of the Front hymn. When they succeeded in occupying the house I was taken to the Security offices.

During the fighting itself, while they had me inside the police car in front of the house, they started searching the neighbouring houses. Out of house next door they took a boy who was resting. They took him without his shoes or shirt, and with the butts of their guns. Because he was a young boy they thought he had to be a member of the Front. That gives you some idea of their impression of how very many people were against them. Then they grabbed that boy and started pistol-whipping him. The boy stumbled, and without even knowing who he was they began shooting and filled him full of bullets. He was left looking like a collander, shot there on the ground. They told me to tell the journalists that the boy was my brother—I could see all this because I was about a meter from where the boy was shot—as if his being my brother could have justified murder, or the way they did it.

From the radio in the squad car I learned that they had also assassinated other comrades. In the other house they didn't succeed in capturing the woman comrade who looked after that boy; she was able to escape. Later I found out she'd managed to escape by the roof, and that she received a lot of solidarity from the people. She had had to remain on the same block. The block was surrounded for about three days and nobody was allowed to leave. She had to spend all that time in one house. The houses were searched but the people protected her. They didn't hand her over, they protected her and introduced her as an occupant of the house. The comrade appeared there by chance, didn't know the family, just jumped down into the first courtyard she could, after going from roof to roof, and they protected her. Only when the Guard went away was she able to leave and rejoin her comrades.

A lot of people were taken prisoner, among them the woman comrade they captured in *las Delicias*; she and her little girl. She

Julio Buitrago who before dying shouted "Long Live Sandino."

was held there for several days with the girl. Later they returned her to her family. In the same way they jailed another comrade who was pregnant, and several other women because of the simple fact of having a relationship with some member of the Front. They locked up comrades totally unconnected with the event.

" He said that day I belonged to them . . . "

In jail, rather, in the same vehicle I was in, they made me lie on the floor and began handling me, lifting up my dress, hitting me with their rifle butts and kicking me. The officer in command of the squad told the other Security agents to be patient, that they were going to the Presidential Palace and there they'd have a good time.

I was taken to the Security offices at about five-thirty or six in the afternoon. They didn't hand me over to the officer of the day—the guard who was to receive me as a prisoner—but the officer told the driver of the vehicle to keep on going to a place they called "The Pines," a place right there in the Presidential Palace, a room adjoining, or near, the kitchen. He said that day I belonged to him, and if I survived then he'd hand me over to the officer of the day.

Before I climbed out of the vehicle they put a hood over my head. They hauled me out by the feet, struck me against the ground and got me up by kicking me . . . After that they started beating me, all of them; I imagine there were about fifteen, there could have been more. Then they hit me with all kinds of things and undressed me. They made me do exercises: squats, horizontal suspensions, lying down, face up and in a sitting position with me touching the tips of my toes.

After doing this for an hour—I was counting the times I did the exercises—a guy said: "No, man, if she was pregnant she'd have miscarried." I realized they thought I was pregnant—I don't know why it should have occurred to them—and had made me do those exercises so I'd have a miscarriage right there.

One of them said: "I saw a movie and couldn't take even fifteen minutes of it . . ." They asked me: "Are you pregnant?" and I said no. They brought me a paper to sign, a blank piece of paper where

they said they were going to write that I wasn't pregnant. I refused
to sign the paper; it could have been used for anything at all.

All that night they did lots of things to me. Another of the
tortures they inflicted was, for example: they took a bench, a
seat without a back, and put me on it totally naked, made me stand
on tiptoe leaning a little forward with knees bent as if to sit down.
Without sitting down, it is impossible to stay in that position for
more than about two or three minutes. They told me to feel with
my hands because underneath me was a bayonet . . . And when I'd
fall I'd be skewered on it. I had to fall. It's something you can't
control. There comes a time when your legs begin to shake and you
fall. You don't let yourself fall, you just fall. When I fell I realized
they had said they put the bayonet there only to torture me, so I'd
hold that position for at least two minutes, making efforts, thinking
I was going to fall and be stuck by that bayonet.

Later they told me they were going to give me electric shocks.
They said they were going to use low voltage because it wasn't a
question of killing me, only hurting me. They made me pick up the
wire but they didn't turn on the current.

The electric goad was something else. We call it the "electric
pike." A "pike" is used by farmers to drive the oxen that pull
wagons. A long pointed stick; there actually are electric pikes to
drive animals into slaughter houses and such. They applied the
pike to my tongue, my nipples and rectum. They also tried to apply
it in my vagina but that was something they weren't able to do
because then I really went at them "with a swift kick" that was so
hard that the pike fell down or I succeeded in grabbing hold of it.
I don't know what mechanism broke, I think a wire connected to
the batteries. It didn't work any more.

A newspaperman had succeeded in approaching the vehicle they
were holding me in. He took my picture and carried off
my tape recorder. He told me to tell him my name, where I was
being held, and if I was hurt. I told him who I was, that I would be
held in *Las Delicias* and wasn't wounded, that I was all right.

Very early the next morning a fellow came and said: "This son
of a bitch didn't talk because she knew she'd had her picture
taken." Before, while I was being tortured, they had said to me:
"What a shame, so young and because she was captured wounded
in combat, well, we couldn't save her!" They said I had to pay for

the death of one of the agents who died on the way to the hospital. That was going to be my end; "on the way to the hospital" I was going to die.

Apparently they had given orders for the international news agencies to publish the news of my death; for example, the AP sent out a cable saying I'd been captured wounded and had died later in the hospital. But they didn't know about the newspaperman. It kept them from assassinating me.

During the interrogation they used the policy of softening-up. First they mistreated me; there was a guy who specialized in this: blows, words, beatings with a club. Then there was another who came and said to the first man: "Let her be, don't hit her, we'll see if good treatment . . . Come here . . . Let me question her, don't keep on mistreating her, she'll shut up more because you've mistreated her so much, this is nonsense. Let me try . . ." Then he put me aside and said: "Look here, as a first condition, let her get dressed. I can't see a woman in that condition."

So they let me dress . . . Meanwhile, the other interrogator, the "bad one," the fellow who played the part of "being bad," said to him: "No, the thing is, this woman has nothing to do with anything." So the "good guy" began to say I should tell him where the other comrades were, what they had done, what the address of the members of the Front leadership was, and where they were. At first I didn't answer any questions, and then the guy said to me: "Look, I want to help you. We won't gain anything if you talk; so many hours have gone by that if you give us an address we'll go there and not find anybody. They will already have gone. Talk so they don't keep beating you."

All this used up a lot of time. I later found out that the one who played the "good" part was a guy named Flores who had studied with me at the Institute. Now he held the rank of lieutenant. I realized it was him because he told me, and once I had the opportunity of seeing his face. Later, one day when he thought I was asleep, he began talking, he was drunk and he told the custodian what they had done to me.

That fellow proposed that I go to bed with him. He said he was going to protect me—it's all part of the softening-up policy. He told me he was only testing me when he had ordered me to eat shit— another woman would have said yes, but he could finally see I was "good." When he understood he really wasn't going to get anything out of me, he said: "Now you see we can't do anything with you; seems as if you want to keep on being beaten . . ."

Another of the torture methods they use is, for example, what they call "Vietnamese." A guy came and said: "Leave her to me, I've just come from a fort—those North American forts they have in the training bases—and I specialized in Vietnamese torture." Then he ordered them to bring a lot of very sharp stones, with sharp edges, the rough ones used in construction. He scattered them on the ground and ordered me to kneel down on them and get up, kneel down and get up. There comes a time when you can't get up. Every time you kneel you get cut with the stones. When you get up some of the stones fall, others don't. He had me doing this for a long time. Every time I kneeled, the stones cut me—sometimes in the same places, sometimes in others. When I couldn't do this any more by myself, two guards, two Security agents, grabbed me and kneeled me down and stood me up.

There were other tortures. They had hurled a tear gas or smoke bomb, which are long, and one of the capsules left was more or less in the shape of a penis. They took that thing and raised my hood a bit, showed it to me and said that since I was already corrupt—because to them, of course, a Communist has to be a degenerate—they were going to stick this into me. And another guy said: "No, man, not if she's going to enjoy it . . ." In other words, what they were trying to do was humiliate me, annoy me.

Then they made me do squats again, totally naked, and placed one of those objects in such a way that each time I squatted it would go into my rectum. They never went so far as to rape me—rather they made use of sex to damage me psychologically and physically. They handled me, tried to put their hands into my vagina. But I did everything possible to attack them. They masturbated in front of me and handled me while doing so.

One day I was sitting down being interrogated, and a fellow came in and asked: "Is this the woman who still hasn't talked?" I think I had already been there for ten days. The custodian answered: "Yes, she's the one who's holding out like a fool." Then he said: "I'm going to examine her, maybe she's a man and you guys haven't realized it. I'm going to look for the "eggs"—she must have been hiding them . . ."

He put his hand between my legs and I grabbed it. I lifted my hood and could see his hand, though not his face, but I saw the hand and a ring. I didn't say a thing at the time, but he let me go because he was scared, and then he said to the one in charge of me that it would be better if I left, that I could "nail" him. In other words, I could identify him. The guy did succeed in putting two fingers in that really scratched me and I began bleeding.

Meanwhile, they had stopped the exercise punishments and had only gone on with the punishments of not letting me sleep or eat. But some fellows arrived who, according to the custodian, didn't follow the Security's "line," yet fulfilled the same function. I almost certainly knew who one of them was but for tactical reasons I never named the one I suspected . . . except to the comrades. They talked and I heard their voices and I heard one voice I recognized. I found out his height and his stature, more or less, by "accidentally" getting close to him and feeling to guess his size. That guy came every night, stripped me, handled me, threw me against the walls and hit me. He used to bring visitors. Once he said: "this is what I want you to see . . ." and ordered the custodian to undress me. When I was undressed he saw I was bleeding and then he said: "No, no, dress her; it's not worth while to see her that way."

And they made a circle, I imagine, and tossed me from one to the other and slapped me. That's how I was able to touch the features of his face. I could see their silhouettes against the light. That's how I succeeded in identifying some of the officials who were there. A few didn't deny it but told me they hadn't participated in anything; that they didn't agree with those methods, that they had "other" methods . . . When I was later taken to court, I accused those men.

When the interrogator arrived, the day after that guy came, he found me completely exhausted. He asked the custodian what had happened because he had given orders not to make me do any more exercises. The custodian told him: "You know that people come here who I can't keep from doing whatever they want." They spoke of the "Gentleman" and said that the "Gentleman's friend" came too. This was how I figured out that Tacho's sons came, or Tacho himself.

Some of the government collaborators also arrived, and they had free access to the Presidential Palace because they carried out tortures on the ground floor where they lived; they had the Office of Security right there. Among the collaborators of the regime I succeeded in identifying was the present minister of labour, Julio Cardoza. I saw that fellow when I was moved from the Security offices to the Police. He tried to hide but when he realized I had seen him he went out and screamed at the agents who were moving me to take me quickly because there were some newspapermen around there. I remember that Cardoza was wearing a striped shirt.

". . . I was able to see an executive briefcase on the table . . ."

On the thirteenth day the interrogator arrived early in the morning. He ordered me to get up to finish the interrogation. That guy told me he'd been at a party and that he'd been taken from the party. He was dead drunk and said some insane things. He asked me: "Why did they give you money?" And before I could say anything, he said: "Well, they gave it to you to buy milk," and he put down: "They gave it to her to buy milk."

I told him it bothered me to talk through the hood. He said I could lift it up a bit, only a bit, to talk. I raised it a little and was able to see a belt buckle he was wearing; it had some gold initials on it. And then, at the same time, I was able to see an executive briefcase on the table, and it had the same initials as the belt buckle. I even succeeded in seeing some papers he had, because he got up to get a cup of coffee very often. He was very drunk.

We finished the declarations in mid-morning of the following day. He told me I was going to be given permission to take a bath and change my clothes. They lead me to "The Pines" to return the clothes they had made off with in the house. First they brought me a suitcase with clothes that weren't mine. Then the man who brought me the clothes went out again and I began to hear snoring. I started to raise the hood and when I had it at a certain height and nobody said anything, I raised it all the way and went to see who that interrogator was. He'd been drunk since the night before and hadn't slept and so was sleeping right there. He was a fellow called Orlando Hislop who was studying economics at the University. I got a good look at him, replaced the hood and went back to the corner they'd left me in.

At once a custodian arrived and took me to another place. Through a fellow who was or is—I don't know—a friend of my papa, and is an official, they tried to convince me to accept a trip out of the country and a scholarship. He told me that in any event if I left and made declarations and accused those men, the only thing I'd get out of it would be to lose my reputation as Nicaragua is a very moral nation, and if I said I'd been naked in front of a few people and had been handled by the Guard, I wasn't going to be worth a thing. I told him it didn't matter, I knew it wasn't so, and that they were the ones without a reputation. One of those who tried to convince me was Moises Sediles; he was Communications Head of the CONDECA, the Central American Army.

"I stayed in jail for six more months. Two years in all."

During the time I was held in Security, there were popular mobilizations demanding that I be given a trial. Then they had to take me to court and I managed to make declarations to a journalist who had remained in the judge's office. He tape recorded my statement. The people demonstrated in front of the Palace of Justice and in the departments; progressive priests, and even persons from the bourgeoisie, protested. Later I was introduced to other journalists and permitted to tell everything that had happened.

Later I found out my papa had been called on and that the head of Security, Samuel Genie, tried to convince him I was totally corrupt, and to prove it he showed him some Marxist books which, according to Genie, I had in my possession. My papa gave his statement to the Guard, and it was accepted.

In jail I was held for some time incommunicado and was accused of the death of that fellow who had been wounded inside the house. I was accused of complicity in the death of the guard on the twentieth of September 1968 and of complicity and concealment in several attacks and "expropriations" that had taken place all through that year. They couldn't make these accusations stand up because the only proof they had was the statements of other prisoners and of Security agents.

The popular mobilizations obliged the magistrates of the court to throw out a large part of the charges. I was tried on charges of homicide, of concealment and complicity in the attack, and of attempting a crime against the Political Constitution of the State. In the trial the Chief of Security was called as a witness to show the written declarations, the statements I had presented to him complaining of the abuses they had committed against me. The interrogator was called as were other officials I had identified. Of course they didn't show up. The jury acquitted me.

I stayed in jail for six more months. Two years in all. I got out on May 12 or 15, 1971, after twenty-nine days of a hunger strike and a popular mobilization at the national level. There were seizures of churches, seizures of study centers, partial work stoppages. That's how thirteen prisoners accused of being members of the Sandinist Front were freed.

" . . . the women in all our oppressed countries . . ."

If we say something about the women who were in jail with me—the regular prisoners—you get some idea of the true condition of the Nicaraguan peasant and proletarian women exploited by the country's ruling class and by imperialism. Actually, about the women in all our oppressed countries.

I reached my cell at about noon; at five in the afternoon I already had news of all my comrades, of the rest of the comrades who were prisoners and were also being punished. I was able to hear about them, and at the same time they were able to know that I was all right so they wouldn't worry about me.

Even the ordinary prisoners invented some voluntary job, like cleaning up the courtyards, to be able to leave their cells and have a chance to communicate with the other inmates for me. They helped me get out of my cell. They invented having to scrub down cells—to do that the prisoner has to be taken out—so I could go into the courtyard and get some sun and see some of my comrades there. They made it possible to communicate with the rest of the comrades every day, with the women from the cell as well as with the children prisoners—there were children there, from the age of five all the way to adults—with the thieves, and people locked up for that kind of crime.

Since I couldn't read the newspapers, they took charge of reading the news and letting me know by means of signals. In this sense the jail wasn't disagreeable for me, it was a very good and very profitable experience—precisely because I was able to get to know those women and especially the children.

They helped me not only to communicate inside the jail, but also with people outside. I could send letters to the newspapers. There was even the case of a prisoner who carried on the work of delivering inside mail. They knew she was the one who carried the mail, so often they stripped her and made her do squats to find out in what part of her body the mail was hidden. And yet for six months this woman brought me mail. I told her I was afraid and not to bring any more letters because it was a long time, six months, and she could be beaten. Those beatings were very brutal.

Most of the prisoners in with me were of peasant stock. Some were city women who had been workers, and had for various reasons gone into prostitution or thievery. Among the prostitutes, most were of peasant stock—not only of peasant stock, many were peasants.

It was customary for the dealers in white women, people in charge of supplying the brothers with women, to go into the countryside, to the mountainous region where the population suffers from hunger, and recruit women supposedly to do housework in the city. They bring peasant girls of thirteen and fourteen to work as "daughters of the house." That variant of slavery . . . These people dedicated to dealing in white women use this cover to recruit young peasant girls, daughters of ruined peasants or of the agricultural proletariat, who are brought to the city and taken directly to the whorehouses. They're forced to participate in that life. They have no right to the part of the payment the madam gives to the other prostitutes. These newcomers arrive without clothes or shoes and are paid with used clothing. They have no right to leave the brothel, nor even to go near the front door.

After the clients leave and the "business" is over, the madam locks up the peasant girl inside the room. Her clothers are taken away so she can't go anywhere. These girls suffer bestial treatment. One of them told me about it; she had been able to escape because a "client" came drunk, and she got out on the pretext of going to the bar to get him a beer or something of that kind, and that's how she was able to escape.

But they went looking for her; she was a peasant. She didn't know the city, didn't know how to work, and they located her easily and took her prisoner. They accused her of stealing nearly a thousand dollars worth of clothing. All she did was take the clothes she had on her back at the moment and one other dress. The clothes didn't even cost five *cordobas*.

The madams of the houses of prostitution carry on their business together with the Guard and the commanders of the barracks and jails. This girl had been lead directly from where she was captured to the jail. She didn't know how to notify her family. She was there nearly three months, until another madam arrived—they go to the jails very often, pick out the youngest and prettiest girls, and pay their fines with the understanding that they have to go and work in the bars they own.

This is a vicious circle. The girls can never leave the place because they don't know the amount that would allow them to cancel the debt imposed on them. They're totally enslaved and frightened because they realize the friendship that exists between the commander and the madam of the whore house.

There were two women there, madams of brothels, who visited the prison frequently. One was the adoptive mother of a corporal who worked there—we called him "The Bird," the same fellow who appeared in the stadium that day—and the other was the official mistress of the head prison warden who at that time was Alesio Gutierrez. These women were continually taking out and putting in girls. They took out the ones they wanted, and when they couldn't report any profit or if the girls rebelled, they put them in by accusing them of any old thing.

They also told me in those whorehouses they gave the girls medicine to keep them from menstruating, so they wouldn't stop earning money a single day. When they became pregnant they made them abort. They corrupted them to such an extent that when they finally left, it was impossible for them to find a way of remaining in any other environment.

Many of the thieves were city women who couldn't find any work. There was the case of a woman taken prisoner accused of robbery. She was an honest worker who did ironing in people's homes. She used to do ironing in the home of a military man but in that house they never paid her the wages she earned with her ironing.

Once she went to the house and told the wife of this guard that if they didn't pay her, she was going to walk off with the ironing. They owed her much more than that pile of ironing was worth. This threat was enough for the woman to be taken. She was taken to court accused of stealing property. They never indicated exactly what had been stolen or that she had stolen anything at all. Now she has a record as a thief. Later, when she was asked for references for some job, she had a police record and was no longer accepted as a worker anywhere.

Some other women who really did steal had been practically servants in the jail and had no other prospects. There was another woman who once left the kind of life she lived and began to work as a domestic—because she didn't know anything else. And then she told me that what she earned in one month of housework she could easily get in a single day by stealing. Not counting the bad treatment she received from her employers and the long hours of work—houseworkers worked nearly twelve or fourteen hours a day, sometimes more—for a salary of a hundred and fifty *cordobas*, when they were well paid, and they had to sweep, clean the house, cook, and at times do the laundry.

This woman had a large family. A mother and four children. She couldn't support her children on a hundred and fifty *cordobas*. Besides, they didn't admit her with her family in those jobs so she was forced to leave that kind of work and devote herself to stealing. Cases of this type were extremely numerous.

There's another kind of prostitution in the country. On account of their low salaries, some workers, to support their families, find themselves obliged to walk the streets on weekends in search of a customer. These are people well aware of the conditions they live in . . . These women are submitted to the worst kind of abuse because since they're not professional prostitutes, as the others are called, they don't have the health card needed in the whorehouse. So these women have to walk the streets and go more or less to the places where men and tourists and those kinds of people hang out at night. They have to fix themselves up to advertise what the men are looking for.

These women are repressed by special patrols that work mainly on weekends when these workers go out. As a general rule the patrols receive some gratuity from the brothel owners. They arrest these women, take away the money they've earned, take some piece of jewelry they're wearing, rape them, and impose very stiff fines.

I had the opportunity of seeing this kind of repression applied to a young girl—it seemed almost as if it was the first time she did this; she was about fifteen or sixteen—and they couldn't find her money because she hadn't earned any and she wasn't wearing anything of value. So they raped her. And it turned out she was a virgin— a"miss," as they say—who hadn't ever done anything of this kind. Several of the guys there calmly raped her.

Prostitution in the country is a problem reaching massive proportions. Salaries in the countryside as well as in the city are very low. In the city a person is supposed to earn a minimum salary, but nevertheless the contractors take advantage of the small demand for labour to pay below this minimum, without the worker's being able to denounce him. They also make use of keeping the worker fearful by means of the monthly act of signing a "rejection" slip. The worker knows that this becomes effective only at the moment when he protests that he is being paid less than his rightful salary. By this kind of maneuvering the boss avoids paying for the seventh day, vacations, and all social benefits, because workers apparently never work one month straight in any industry. There are workers who sign the "rejection" slip every week. It is this situation that makes the proletarian woman resort to prostitution or robbery every time.

It's worse in the countryside. There they don't respect any minimum salary. In addition to which in the country there's more discrimination against women. They maintain that women don't work as well as men. It isn't true, because a peasant woman skilled in gathering cotton or picking coffee does as well as a man. If it weren't so, women wouldn't be hired. But her work is paid quite a bit below its worth. A male worker who picks coffee, for one container of coffee beans—there's no fixed price—earns up to four, five, or six dollars. For the same work a woman earns two dollars, a much lower amount than is earned by a man.

"children are almost exclusively a concern of the mother . . ."

All the prisoners joined in the hunger strikes we carried out in prison so we would be set free. The mothers too: our mothers, the mothers of condemned comrades, mothers of dead comrades, sisters, representatives of political organizations, and of the student movement. The struggle for the freeing of the prisoners and the solidarity and support for the prisoners was a struggle headed by women.

Why do I believe that women take a greater part in this type of thing? Given the kind of society we have where children are almost exclusively a concern of the mother, the child is the mother's problem. When he or she has to study or when they have some kind of conflict it's the mother who faces it because the man in this society, in a society like ours, doesn't participate in any practical sense in the upbringing of his child. In Nicaragua there are many cases—though not all, of course—in which those serving in the Front find solidarity for their militant activities in their mothers. Many times the weight of the campaigns for freeing the imprisoned comrades falls on them.

In 1973 there was one of the greatest campaigns for freedom of and solidarity with the Sandinist Front prisoners. A hunger strike was started demanding the freedom of comrade Francisco Ramirez Urbina, an ex-guard who had given his rifle to the Front. It also demanded freedom for a comrade who wasn't a member of the Organization, professor Efrain Nortlewalton, a professor from the University of El Salvador who had been exiled to our country right after that university's military occupation. He was arrested by the immigration authorities and had no possibility of being freed unless there was strong popular pressure. So the jailed comrades went on an indefinite hunger strike until the persons mentioned were given their freedom. The campaign for the prisoners was a massive one. First the prisoners went on a hunger strike, and then the student movement, the FER and the neighbourhood organizations made public the prionsers' demand and made common cause with them. The struggle for better living conditions and the struggle against the government's repression against the popular sectors was added to the demand for the comrade's freedom.

After doing propaganda around the strike, the mothers, together with some students, seized a church, the Church of the Holy Faith in Managua. They also went on a hunger strike and popular meetings were held around the church, in which the mothers took part, explaining why their sons and daughters were imprisoned and the why and wherefore of the Front struggle. They explained the reasons for the conditions the people faced, the oppression, hunger and ignorance in which the Nicaraguan people live. They also lit small bonfires at night around a big fire, recited revolutionary poems and read proclamations. There were recitals and theatrical presentations. There were bonfires not only around the church where the mothers were, but also in other sections, mainly in the neighbourhoods.

Churches were taken over in other departments as well. After each fire there were demonstrations. The demonstrations were composed principally of townspeople but there were also high school and university students, professional persons and people of the opposition petty bourgeoisie.

There were meetings held in the open air and on the streets which were attended mostly by the common people. Every work sector or social sector talked and participated in the meetings—the workers, the domestic employees, representatives of the native quarters, representatives of the neighbourhoods, nurses, students, people from the University union and in the union of University professors. In short, the participation was enormous.

At night we burned effigies that symbolized repressive elements. This is a tradition of the Nicaraguan people—representing the persons who repress or exploit them. This is done by means of an effigy that is paraded through the city before being burned. At the meetings the comrades spread the names and life histories of the martyrs of the Sandinist Front. They also made known Sandino's struggle and its continuation through the struggle of the Front.

" . . . My son, they'll kill the two of us, but they won't take you away."

Theatrical themes are based on administrative corruption and the repressive elements of the Guard and the Security officers. These theatrical sessions were extremely important. The Nicaraguan people love theater and of course love popular theater. The Nicaraguan people have a great theatrical tradition, a tradition which is still preserved, in spite of the fact that imperialist cultural penetration has attempted to destroy it.

Theatrical traditions are preserved and that's why the general public participates. They enjoy this theater, and the Organization, by means of the student movement, has organized theatrical groups whose job it is to take to the various neighbourhoods representations of their problems.

When the Subtiavan Indians—an indigenous group in Leon— had problems with the land, the student theater went to the Subtiavan district and put on a play based on the land problem. And in the struggle to free the prisoners, they took plays to the neighbourhoods—and to as many places as possible—that had to do with the condition of people's lives, the oppression they experience, the repression of the Guard, the economic situation— which after all is the situation against which those jailed comrades are fighting.

Using popular theater as a way of coming into a district, of politicizing it, as a vehicle of propaganda, has produced great results in Nicaragua. Theater has the advantage of action—I don't know if I'm explaining this well but I mean in a play you can explain with talking and gestures. And when these plays present the problems the people are living, the possibility of understanding is even greater . . . Without affectation, sometimes without make-up or scenery—there are even cases where the actors don't have to learn their lines by heart—the actors catch on to the idea, to the orientation of the dialogue, and the lines come out naturally.

I remember an experience in 1971 or 1972. There was a play about the Sandinist Front of National Liberation. It was during a campaign to free the prisoners. That play showed a Front cell meeting surprised by the Guard. The play was put on in a Managua neighbourhood without scenery. The neighbours, the public, were gathered around the place where the "cell was meeting." And when the "Guard" broke in they surrounded the public and tried to push the people aside to reach the "cell." The public ran and screamed but one woman, instead of running away, rushed impetuously at the "actors" and succeeded in grabbing a comrade and without letting him go, said: " . . . My son, they'll kill the two of us, but they won't take you away." It took a lot of doing to convince the people that "the Guard" was part of the theatrical group. The people thought it was the real Guard coming to break up an FER play.

Progressive singers and poets took part in these cultural events around the freeing of prisoners. One of the sectors of the population that figured prominently in the struggle was the market women. These comrades would confront the Guard directly. Most of them were women, with some men. They confronted the Guard directly to lift the siege that was set up at the Leon cathedral where there was a hunger strike going on by some students and some representatives of the workers' movement and the native communities. When those comrades lifted the siege, they succeeded in taking lemons and some little things to eat to the people there. In other words, the Guard failed to make the siege effective. The people always managed to make fun of those guards.

The people also created centers of resistance in the city. These centers were moveable so they could easily be thinned out, to fool the Guard . . . There weren't big groups of people resisting, but little groups scattered all over the city in such a way that the Guard couldn't concentrate their forces on any one group.

Houses in the city were turned into refuges. The people *en masse* supported this campaign and protected the demonstrators. Some three thousand persons were mobilized every day—maybe more. The demonstrations increased progressively from morning till night. They carried placards with anti-Somoza, anti-bourgeoisie, anti-imperialist slogans painted on them.

Small demonstrations all over the city joined others at a prearranged time and formed one single demonstration. When the small demonstrations were formed at various points in the city, they went to the homes of the Somoza deputies, to the homes of the Somoza leaders, the agents of repression, the Somoza allies, and held meetings to denounce these people.

The important thing about this campaign was that it wasn't limited to the problem of the prisoners who had to be set free—to the injustice of having a man held for more than five years without any charge—but it was focussed on the situation of the people, their living conditions, the increasing scarcities of life, the repression in the mountains and in the cities. The whys and wherefores of this were clearly explained.

These demonstrations started in the neighbourhoods and converged toward the city's center. It was remarkable how the people mobilized in spite of the threat of the Guard, and how they resisted. The people spontaneously went out into the streets, and in the face of the Guard those same people organized demonstrations and resistance. One of the focal points of the demonstrations was the Social Club. Then there were the churches where the bourgeoisie attended their religious services. The students and the people of Leon went on a long walk to Managua—some ninety kilometers—where the bourgeoisie and the government were going to hold a military Mass which would be attended, they knew, by Somoza . . .

"I talked about the women, and how they struggle . . ."

I talked about the women, and how they struggle—even the mothers, many of whom weren't militants or participants in the struggle until their sons or daughters fell prisoner or were assassinated . . . Among the mothers fighting today is Dona Santos, mother of Julio Buitrago.

I met comrade Julio Buitrago at the Institute. Julio also got his bachelor's degree in the Ramirez Goyena. He arrived there probably in 1958 or 1959. Julio was a comrade with a very strong character, a person who could be called unswerving. Julio was a guy who had had great difficulty being able to study. His mother was a working woman. Julio was "illegitimate" and his mother had to work all the time to be able to support him.

He told me how his mother had to suffer the consequences of having a child without being married, how she'd been rejected even by her own family and how, with that son, she had to face great difficulties, mainly economic, because with a child it was very hard to find work. He told me that when he was very young, he must have been ten, he had to go and sell newspapers, chewing gum and candy at the entrances to movie houses. Yet Julio's mother was a person who sacrificed herself all the time and always worked so he could get ahead, so he could excel and be able to study. That's how Julio got his BA.

During his years as a student at the Ramirez Goyena, he was entirely dedicated to his studies and to his work in the student movement. Julio was outstanding in organizational work at the Ramirez Goyena Student Center. He was a leader in that school all the time. He also served in Patriotic Youth. Then Julio went on to the University and devoted himself to working in the student movement at the University, but didn't ignore his high school political work. He continued to attempt to organize a federation of high school students. Julio joined the Sandinist Front when very young, when he was scarcely twenty. He played an active part in it and became a member of the National Administration.

In my conversations with Julio I was able to realize the great respect, the great admiration he had for women. For Julio every woman, any woman—and more so if she was a comrade—was like the image of his mother. He told me he couldn't see a woman suffer or be in need because it made him think of his mother.

Julio always told me that one of the things that worried him most was that his mother, Dona Santos, probably wouldn't be able to bear the sorrow of his death, that the day that happened, she'd die too. At times he told me he was concerned that his mother, due to the love he felt for her, was a little selfish and had done everything possible to keep Julio from participating so openly.

She agreed with Julio's being an opponent of the government and being against Somoza, but at first she didn't want Julio to commit himself entirely. Nevertheless he never stopped participating or carrying out any activity simply because his mother didn't want him to. Julio discussed this with me and said he had wanted his mother to participate alongside him.

When Julio went into hiding, Dona Santos accepted the situation. She knew her son would never give up, and she respected his determination. It's one of her most positive traits: that great respect she had for her son's decision.

When Julio died, Dona Santos survived. And not only did she survive and bear her sorrow at the death of her son, but she changed radically. Dona was a mother worthy of a Sandinist martyr. She went to the meetings, took part in the struggle to free the prisoners, went to many assemblies with the mothers of other imprisoned comrades, and helped plan popular campaigns. Dona Santos attended student congresses at the high school level where homage was being paid to Julio. Dona Santos took into her hands the flag left by Julio when he died, and in some way her son was continuing the struggle through her.

This is something I wished were possible, that Julio for a moment could know his mother's attitude. It would be really marvellous if he could know that his mother didn't die, nor did she stay calmly at home; she took up the struggle, dedicated to making him live on, to keeping Julio's image alive through her participation.

"My own mother . . ."

My own mother . . . She was always steadfast. Steadfast in the sense that she never pressured me or did anything at all to make me stop participating, even when it put her family in economic straits. And by the time I returned from the Soviet Union, she had separated from my papa—mainly because of his negative attitude to my militant activity. From then on my mother's family cut off their help. My mama had many money problems. Since then she had to work to live. She sewed. And my sisters, who were already grown up, worked. They helped a little. But her means of subsistence were minimal.

Her family put pressure on her by withholding their aid so she couldn't give me any. At one time, someone in the family even said that my mama was in a bad economic situation because she was surely giving all her money to me, that my mama was sacrificing her other daughters so I could be a militant.

Besides, my mama was the one taking care of my son and they said—her family said—that if my mama left him with me it would be an obstacle to my militancy. I would have to "face facts" in order to support him and wouldn't possibly be able to participate in the Organization.

Yet faced with all kinds of pressures she always stood firm until her family gave in. Years later, after it was discovered that she had terminal cancer, they gave her some land and stopped pressuring her. During her sickness she never stopped helping me and doing everything possible to take part in our struggle.

Even when she was sick and unable to move, she made my papa take her on a cot to Police Headquarters—this was in 1971—to see that my order of freedom was really carried out by the judge. When I left the prison she was very ill.

She died in December of 1972. She always used to tell me that it was a disgrace, that she was of no use any more, because she couldn't even take charge of raising my son, and that it was going to be harder for me to work. This was on her mind all the time; even just before she died she was harping on it; she felt bad because she couldn't even take care of the boy.

" . . . he had had a single dream in his life . . ."

I met Leonel in 1968. At the time I didn't know he was Leonel Rugama. We met at a house where he came to do some shooting, some military exercises. At that time my comrade, Ricardo, pointed out to me that Leonel, in spite of having poor eyesight—he wore glasses—had a very good aim. Later I saw him at another house, and I remembered that he was the same comrade who had such good aim. In those days I was reading a book of poems by Cesar Vallejo, and Leonel talked to me about Vallejo, and we began to talk about Vallejo's poetry and some essays. After that he continued coming to that house every weekend. We always discussed literature. Together we revised some poems of my comrade, the first poems Ricardo wrote in jail, which were published in the newspaper *The Student*.

Leonel loved to hear popular tales, stories of the people, and was very much interested in knowing stories told in the countryside. He asked me to tell him about my childhood. What games did I play? So I told him they said there was a goblin in my house, a "good goblin," and this goblin used to bring us presents, caramels, many things; that it was a question of my grandmother or my mama putting them in definite places in the house, under our pillows when we were asleep, or under our plates . . . These things made our childhood pleasant.

When I told this to Leonel, he told me that in his house they were so poor that there weren't any "good goblins," that the goblins in his house were "scoffing goblins," goblins that threw stones, hid toys he made himself out of broken pieces of wood or oat cans.

He always talked about his dear little grandmother. He told me he used to gather some seeds we called "tears of St. Peter." The peasants make necklaces and rosaries out of these seeds. He liked "tears of St. Peter" rosaries a lot because he said they reminded him of his grandmother.

Leonel was a very simple person and at the same time surprising. Nobody who talked with him could imagine he was Leonel Rugama, the writer of the essay "The Student and Revolution," that had earned him a prize in 1968 in a competition in honour of comrade Casimiro Sotelo. Leonel was then in his first year at the University. Much less could it be imagined that he was the author of the poem "The Earth is a Satellite of the Moon."

He also liked to be told dreams and asked me to tell him mine. When I told him I dreamed in colour, he laughed and said it was because I had had a very happy childhood and so could dream in colour, but that most of the people of the country dreamed in black and white. He told me he had had a single dream in his life and it had been in black and white, because this thing of colours in dreams was like at the movies; the most expensive movies were in colour and the cheapest or worst in black and white. He was always making observations on the difference in the lives of the powerful classes and the lives of the ordinary people. He made me see how this is there even in dreams, in games, in a person's expression.

I have no exact memory of when I found out he was Leonel Rugama, but already by January 15, 1970 when the Guard assassinated him, I knew it was Leonel, and . . . Even then Leonel was surprising. When from outside of the house the Guard demanded that he surrender, he answered them: "Surrender your mother, you great big son of a bitch!"

That day, January 15, 1970, was one of the cruelest days I can remember in the prison. The place where Leonel was assassinated was quite nearby. At about two in the afternoon we heard the first shots, and we could see there was some strange activity in the barracks.

They locked up all the prisoners who were around the courtyard whose jobs were cleaning and kitchen work. And they reinforced the posts and stationed a guard at the door of the women's cell block with an order that nobody go near the door. At first I thought it was an "expropriation," inasmuch as there was a bank branch and the Pepsi-Cola plant less than a block from the command post. I was happy. But when I heard more intense shooting and airplanes overhead and shots fired from half-tracks, then I realized a battle was going on and I despaired at my impotence and felt more of a prisoner than ever.

At that moment the guards from the barracks became almost hysterical. And the corporal, the fellow we called "The Bird," came to the cell door and said to one of the women, who was known for mistreating the common prisoners, that he was going to bring in about four Sandinists.

It wasn't until the next day that I realized they had assassinated the comrades and that among them was Leonel.

"He began participating while still a child."

Besides Leonel, they killed Mauricio Hernandez and Roger Nunez. Roger was one of the youngest comrades of the Organization. He began participating while still a child. He wasn't even fifteen. In 1967 he was arrested along with his mother, comrade Aurora Nunez. We in the Organization called her "the little mother" because she sometimes acted like the mother of many of the comrades. She was taken because a machine gun was found in her house. Both Roger and his mother were arrested, and Roger wasn't even fifteen. The boy was tortured very brutally and condemned in spite of being a minor who couldn't be judged legally in the common courts. Roger was in prison nearly six months, left the jail and definitively joined the Organization, till he was killed in January 1970.

In February and March of that year, in the mountains of the north, in Zinica, a guerrilla camp was discovered. In it were peasant women who were very valuable for the group's survival. These comrades did exploratory work that permitted the guerrillas to evade the net spread around them. The main body of the group was made up of rural people, peasantry, and represented a continuation of the political work done by the Pancasan guerrillas. At that time the Guard carried out a massacre in the mountains of Yaosea where they killed entire families.

"She was one of those comrades who lifted people's spirits, who strengthened . . ."

Also in prison, in April of 1970, I learned of the death of Luisa Amanda Espinosa. I was taken out of my cell at about six in the evening without any explanation and when I reached the office of the chief warden I noticed a sense of expectation in the people there and I became alarmed.

At first I thought it was a question of the hunger strike we had planned for that day. The chief warden took out a newspaper and suddenly handed it to me, as if wanting to surprise me. Of course it did surprise me because I recognized right away the name of Enrique Lorente; I read the text of the news item and found that they hadn't recognized the dead woman comrade, but said it was probably a comrade I knew since they were sure the blouse she was wearing had been mine. I don't know where they made up that story. I told them I didn't know her and was sorry I didn't.

Months later a guard came to the prison and said he had been in the fight where Luisa Amanda and Enrique were killed, and this guard told me he never could have imagined that a woman could fight the way she did. I didn't know Luisa Amanda personally, but I knew about her from accounts that other comrades gave me. She was one of those comrades who lifted people's spirits, who strengthened . . .

In 1963 a cell of the FSLN rented a room in one of Managua's
proletarian districts. This room belonged to Luisa Amanda's aunt.
Comrades Jorge Navarro and Marvin Gerrero lived in the house.
There was a girl there, barely eleven years old, who out of curiosity
leaned out the window of the room. That was the beginning of a
relationship between Luisa Amanda and the revolutionaries.
Navarro, who played the guitar and accordion, used to sing
revolutionary songs to her and talk about the sufferings of the
children in our country.

Navarro died in the mountains with the guerrillas of Bocay in
1963, but the house continued to be visited by Sandinist
revolutionaries, among them Rigoberto Cruz, known in the
mountains of Matagalpa as Pablo Ubeda. Rigoberto fell in combat
in Pancasan in 1967. Luisa Amanda's aunt joined the Organization
by way of Rigoberto, as a collaborator.

In 1969 Luisa Amanda worked with the SNEN (National Service
for the Eradication of Malaria). Through this work she became
acquainted with the Nicaraguan countryside. When she was
working in the valley of San Jose de Cusmapa, a National Guard
detailed to the place tried to rape her, and her response after a
long struggle was to stab him to death. She went back to her
house in Managua and told the comrades of the FSLN what had
happened.

The comrades decided to take her into hiding, and in her new
situation she carried out jobs of contact, mail and vigilance, and
took on the responsibilities of a safe house—a hideout. Right
after the deaths of Julio Buitrago and other comrades, and my
arrest, she was taken to Leon, the country's second city, where she
continued to do outstanding work in the jobs already mentioned.

On April 3, 1970, she was found in the streets of Leon, in the
company of comrade Enrique Lorente. The repression had
intensified there. The day before, Lieutenant Ernesto Abaunza, a
gumshoe of the regime, had been executed.

When Luisa Amanda and Lorente were tracked down, there was
an unequal fight with patrols from the Guard in Managua. Lorente
fell dead and Luisa picked up his gun. She wounded a Security
agent and later she herself was wounded and captured. A Guard
jeep took her away. She was tortured by Ronald Sampson (then
lieutenant, now captain) and assassinated moments afterwards.

This young heroine, the first Nicaraguan woman to die in combat in this new stage of our struggle wrote the following which we succeeded in rescuing from the hands of the Office of Security:

I don't want this house of psychedelic colours,
I want the peasant's hut,
I want to be beside the peasant.

Lorente and Rigoberto Cruz were representative of working class men in our people's organized struggle. Lorente joined the ranks of the FSLN at the end of 1963 when he was a textile worker in the Gadala Maria mills. He had started the job of organizing the textile workers but was repressed and dismissed from the work center because of his political work. After that he went into the ranks of our Organization full time. People in Managua were left with good memories of his work in the neighbourhoods where he took part in organizing the People's Civic Committees which were initiated by the Front as a means of linking us to the working masses. He later went into hiding; traces of his work were left in Leon, Esteli, Granada, and the mountains of Zinica.

"The number of students who have died for the Nicaraguan revolution is very great."

I left prison in May 1971 and entered the University . . .

The proletarian classes have little access to education—often they can't even get to finish the primary grades. Families need the labour of all—including the children—in order to survive. Only a very small number of the children of the proletariat ever reach university. The petty bourgeoisie and some children of the qualified workers who have a few more resources can get to the University though they have to study in the country and can't go abroad. The highest strata of the petty bourgeoisie—those most closely allied with the government and the oligarchic or land-owning or industrial bourgeoisie—go abroad to study or, after receiving their B.Sc or B.A. degrees make a speciality of administering their wealth, their land or their companies.

The students, because of their privileged position in the country,

because of their access to culture and knowledge of the
revolutionary experiences of other countries, have often been the
first to commit themselves to revolutionary theories. Study at the
University pushes them toward revolutionary consciousness. From
the beginning of the Sandinist struggle—in the days of
Sandino—students have mobilizied and participated in the
struggle. The struggles of the student movement have been
answered by the most brutal repression on the part of the
government. The students, as students and as allies of the
proletarian class, have been repressed by the regime on various
occasions: in 1944, in the student massacre of 1959, and later in
1960 when they demonstrated to commemorate the July 23, 1959,
massacre.

Since 1960, every July twenty-third, the students have suffered
repression. Year after year there are arrests and shootings. In
spite of the fact that the Guard has been using more refined
methods of repression—it is making use of training acquired in the
Canal Zone where they learn special techniques for putting down
demonstrations—the student body and other sectors of the
Nicaraguan people participate. They participate knowing they are
going to be attacked.

And the mothers of the martyrs of July 23, 1959, also
participate, leading the demonstrations. One of the women most
distinguished for her participation is the mother of the student
Jose Rubi. Jose was one of those killed on July 23 in 1959. The
name of this comrade is Teodora Somarriba Rubi. Jose was her
only son though she has one daughter. Jose was able to study at
the University because of the great sacrifices she made. She's a
mother from the common people who worked to keep her son in
University. She said it was her "one hope." Ever since Jose was
assassinated she has become more and more involved with the
revolutionary movement. She's been taking part not only in the
demonstrations that commemorate the massacre, but also in the
campaigns to free political prisoners, and in demonstrations
against the Somoza dictatorship. She's been showing more and
more enthusiasm which, instead of diminishing with the years,
increases. It's really incredible to see. Once she said that as long
as the Somozas are alive, she can't die, that she'll die the day the
Somoza regime falls. Meanwhile, she says, she has a moral

agreement with her son to keep on living so that she can struggle.

The number of the students who have died for the Nicaraguan revolution is very great. I could give you a long list of comrades: we have Oscar Danilo Rosales, a graduate of medical school; Silvio Mayorga, a law student; Francisco Moreno, a high school student—the one who as a child lived opposite my house in Matagalpa; Julio Buitrago, also a law student, in his third year; comrade Casimiro Sotelo, in his last year of law school; Jorge Navarro who died in 1963, also a university student; Modesto Duarte who died in the 1963 Bocay guerrilla action; and Mauricio, Modesto's brother, assassinated in January 1975 in Jinotepe, in the repression let loose by the dictatorship after the commando action of last December. The list goes on. The students have won the people's respect.

The Nicaraguan worker sees both student and peasant as his ally. The student movement participates in the people's struggle—not just as isolated students but in the movement as a whole . . .

" . . . the people who normally drank milk . . . couldn't buy it even for their children."

The student movement took an active part in the 1972 campaign against the increases in the prices of milk and gasoline. All through 1972, in the early months and even in the last months of 1971, a massive campaign was mounted against the high cost of milk and gasoline. The price of milk was rising exorbitantly, without any justification—except that it was the nature of the system itself, which found no other way out of its contradictions. The milk monopoly is one of the monopolies in which the Somozas have part of their capital invested. Milk is a food the common people don't have access to, the proletarian people really haven't the means to buy milk.

Rising gasoline prices also hit the majority of the people, especially the working class. It affects all those who use public transportation vehicles as well as the taxi drivers who own their own vehicles. Increased gasoline prices mean higher transportation costs.

These two struggles were carried out together and there were massive demonstrations in all the sectors affected. In this campaign the student movement detailed all the activist teams to work in the marginal neighbourhoods, organizing them to struggle against the dairies and gasoline processors, and against the government which through taxes on these products allows the dairies and service stations to raise the prices.

The campaign, as well as organizing the popular sectors and mobilizing the entire population around this problem which strikes directly at the Nicaraguan family, also did studies which showed the enormous amount of money obtained by the milk companies. They showed how these companies exploit not only the consuming public but the small milk producers as well, forcing them out of the market, how they were preventing the people—by passing prohibitive laws—from being able to drink fresh milk, how the quality of these milk products wasn't regulated, and all too often was dangerous to their health. The studies showed clearly that feeding the people was not a priority of the milk companies.

The campaign was aimed at an immediate problem. The price of milk rose so high that the people who normally drank milk, who aren't the workers but the middle classes, couldn't buy it even for their children. And gasoline: raising the price of public transportation meant increasing hardships for workers. There were cases of construction workers, for example, who earned two hundred odd *cordobas*—a salary that for a construction worker in those days was good—and spent from a hundred and fifty to two hundred on bus fare.

The campaign lasted a long time and when it was over several marginal neighbourhoods were organized. Until this time large sections of the working class didn't have a community or neighbourhood council. They organized around this problem and then the Front continued working in the neighbourhoods to improve conditions. Once the neighbourhoods were organized we were able to struggle for improved living conditions, for the establishment of clinics where people could receive free medical attention, for lighting systems and potable water (nearly all the marginal districts in the capital have no water). Struggles were organized around education—children in these districts had to go far away if they were to attend school. The organizations took up all the many different problems people in the community faced.

In 1970 or the end of 1969, there was a strike at the national level of the public sector. This strike lasted a long time; the teachers relieved of their jobs—many who had taken part in the strike were fired—brought a suit against the ministry of education. There was no precedent for resolving the problem. The student movement took a very active part in that strike. Its teams, through the highest administrative agency, the University Center, helped support that strike, sending teams for propaganda work to mobilize the masses.

" . . . the spectacle was horrible."

The earthquake sharpened the crisis the country was already undergoing. There was an enormous quantity of workers unemployed. The peasant population in the cities had greatly increased. Forced from their lands they had come to the city in search of work . . . Private enterprise was unhappy because it took so small a part in looting the public treasury.

The earthquake resulted in intensifying this whole situation. It left the poorest people in the country poverty-stricken. People couldn't even afford to build a house for a minimum of security. The small producers were also very much affected. Heavy industry suffered on a smaller scale. In the capital, the food and housing shortage, the health problem and unemployment all became more acute. Hospitals were destroyed or limited in their services . . . This was especially serious because all economic activity is concentrated in Managua, the capital, because though Managua doesn't have much agricultural production it's surrounded by industry.

I wasn't in Managua when the earthquake struck—the first minutes of December 23, 1972. My mother had died two or three days before, and I had moved back to my town, to Matagalpa. Yet it was felt there, even in Matagalpa. I immediately tried to find some way of moving to Managua.

When I arrived, the spectacle was horrible. Before I got there you could see that the whole city was in flames. It had burned up. The districts at the entrance to Managua are very poor—the marginal districts—and when we entered the city they were razed to the ground. It made quite an impression seeing whole families sitting on the ground at the edge of what had been their homes, on the sidewalks, some with their dead beside them, and apparently totally indifferent. It was as if they too were dead.

It was horrible. It was my lot to witness the case of a family that was able to get out of the house during the first tremor—there were two. After the first shock was over the lady of the house went in again—she had taken out all her children—to look for a blanket to cover them, and she didn't realize that a little girl of seven had entered with her. The second tremor came and finished knocking down what the first one had left weak. The lady succeeded in running out but since she didn't know that the child was inside, she didn't look for her. When I arrived, the lady was sitting down and beside her lay the body of the little girl, totally decapitated. A wall had fallen on her head. She had only the little body.

After I went and verified the damage done to my house, and took out some books we had there, I went to the house of a few comrades and came across the father of a comrade, who had obtained a cart in which he carried four or five bodies: his mother, a sister, an aunt—he threw them all together and he himself was pulling the cart to see that his dead would be buried.

There were many horrors . . .

The people lived in terror. They didn't know what was going to happen. There was talk of martial law, and the Nicaraguan people knew martial law meant that the Guard had the right to kill anyone in the street.

There were cases of killings by the Guard. For example, the next morning the dairies distributed some leftover milk to the neighbourhoods because it was going sour on them. The people clung to the milk trucks—they hadn't slept, eaten or drunk anything . . . In one neighbourhood the people were clinging to a milk truck that had come to dole out milk, and the Guard began shooting, killing a few people. That's how they restored order.

Something else that terrorized the people was the presence of the US Army. Right after the earthquake, the US Army mobilized forces from the Canal Zone and practically occupied the country. *Gringo* police went through the streets of Managua giving orders. This presented problems because they didn't speak Spanish and so had no way of asking anyone what he or she was doing. The order was to fire at anyone they found in the rubble.

The *gringo* police also carried special flame throwers for burning the bodies. That was something that had a great impact on the Nicaraguan people, because many people hadn't had a chance to bury their dead, and hadn't even been able to extricate them from the rubble because the Guard wouldn't let them. And those *gringos*, just like they did in the 1931 earthquake, burned a lot of bodies—you could smell the odour of burning flesh all over the city.

One of the first places they restored was the United States Embassy which had beeen totally destroyed. In two days it was as clean as if nothing had happened. I imagine it was because to see that place in a state of total destruction would give an impression of the impotence of Yankee imperialism.

The other building they concentrated their energies on was the Aviation Jail. It had disappeared. It was a very old building where many prisoners died—some crushed by the earthquake, and others who had succeeded in escaping through the gaping cracks in the walls machine gunned by the Guard. A lot of bodies were burned there. You couldn't pass by, the odour of burned flesh was so strong. By the end of that very week there was no longer any trace. All signs of destruction, of repression, and of oppression of the people, had been made to disappear. It's my idea that they did those things to try to take away the image of the weakness of their jails. Then international aid began to arrive. You could see how the popular sectors had had to ask for pieces of wood, cardboard boxes, tin cans or pieces of zinc, to make roofs they could live under; and how the mansions, the big houses bordered by large gardens, which had been left almost intact because of their solid construction, had been turned into campaign headquarters donated by the different countries . . .

There was also looting. In Chinendega there was the case of a high government official who had a store in the cellar of a ranch house. It was stocked with all the items of the Casa Mantica. The Casa Mantica is a huge store selling nothing but luxury items. The Guard, the high officialdom dedicated to plunder, looted the cellars of the Manticas. The Mantica family belongs to the opposition bourgeoisie. On that same plantation, along with all those articles from the Casa Mantica, were foodstuffs that had been donated by other nations for the Nicaraguan people.

The United States government donated some wooden houses with a year or two of life. This was called "Program of the Americas." These houses were put up in the outlying districts. They had no foundations, were temporary, and were donated to the neighbourhoods of the INVI, the Housing Institute. To assemble those houses the INVI needed land. Cornelio Hueck, president of the House of Deputies, bought some poor land for $70,000 and immediately turned it over to the INVI for $700,000. This provoked one of many similar scandals in the country.

The Housing Institute houses are the biggest swindle laid on our people. They're houses that are sold or appraised after you give a down payment and a monthly installment. The grantee pays three or even four times their price. It takes about thirty or forty years to own them outright. The construction is very poor and they are houses that cost no more than fourteen or fifteen thousand dollars—the most expensive for the size—yet they're appraised for thirty or forty thousand dollars. So people live in these houses made of pine—a very poor quality wood—that last a year or two, a donation from the United States.

These houses had no light, no water, no streets, not even a minimum amount of the conveniences necessary for anyone to be able to live in them. The Housing Institute located people in the houses and began to charge monthly payments—rent for houses donated by the North American government to the people.

They started to build streets, put in light and then charge for the light, streets and a sewer system . . . And of course epidemics began to spread in these colonies because there were no latrines or adequate places for toilets. What they did do was dig very shallow holes, and the flies spread all kinds of diseases there. Besides, these districts were very near the lake, a very unhealthy spot.

The people refused to pay rent for these temporary houses because they had to keep on paying for their houses in the neighbourhoods that had been destroyed. Even now the INVI is rebuilding the houses in its districts . . . Now, in 1975 . . .

It is very interesting to compare Cuban and North American aid. Cuban aid was the most effective the country received, so the country was forced to accept it. It couldn't refuse. Absolutely not.

The Cuban Revolution built a hospital that gave daily attention to an enormous number of people. It was one of the most complete hospitals. It gave out medicines and even food to the people who went there. Of course the first thing the government did was place a guard outside, to control the people who were going to receive assistance in that hospital.

There was quite a contrast between the hospital put up by the Cubans and the North American one. The Cuban comrades built theirs in the eastern sector, one of the poorest and most densely populated, in that way being able to serve the people who really needed it. The *gringo* hospital was located in back of one of the Somoza ranches, where Somoza lives and where the Guard and Security offices were located. It's a thinly populated area, where the inhabitants are bourgeois. In this section isolated from the needy population and near the Somozas, it looked like a monstrous umbrella, a gigantic tent put up by the *gringos* to protect the Somozas.

This *gringo* hospital was not effective. People weren't going to go near where the Guard had its offices. They themselves recognized the fact. I read an editorial from a North American newspaper where they said this hospital had been built in a section where the people weren't going to go because of distance and the presence of the Guard.

The Nicaraguan people never went near the Guard voluntarily, only when forced. The area where the Americans had installed their hospital gave the impression of a concentration camp, because it was strictly watched over, with guards posted every five or ten meters around *El Retiro*, the Somoza ranch where they took all the people the Guard conscripted to clean up the rubble from the earthquake. There weren't any houses there, not even wooden jails. They slept piled up outdoors in all kinds of weather; they were workers forcibly recruited into that civil corps, later to become the National Guard . . .

To recruit these people the Guard went out to the settlements, mainly to the north and Carazo, and there they collected all the young able men they could find. They organized them under the title of "Civil Reconstruction Corps." Of course they were given a salary, but in the years 1973 and 1974 protests for lack of pay mounted. The people had a horror of being enrolled, because it was rumoured they would be militarized.

International aid was controlled by the National Emergency Committee. Not long ago I read in a newspaper how near the lake an enormous quantity of foodstuffs that had gone bad were burned, while the population had practically nothing to eat because of the high cost of the basic cereal products . . .

The earthquake figures aren't very complete but they calculate about twenty or thirty thousand dead . . . Maybe more. I believe more. And people with trauma: that's incalculable because it doesn't come till later. Besides, in a country where not much attention is paid to health, the psychiatric problems caused by the earthquake can't possibly be counted . . . Almost 100 per cent of the marginal population lost their houses. That was total destruction, whole neighbourhoods flattened . . .

The earthquake was a "business" for some. It happened that City Planning ordered the owners of real property to keep their places clean. These were plots surrounding the city. Huge plots. The ones that didn't belong to Somoza belonged to his relatives or friends, or his guards—and also to other oligarchs opposed to the Somozas . . . Cleaning up these pieces of land cost money. But since they belonged to all these people, they took advantage of those who had to eat, mainly old women. Women had to clean up these areas in exchange for the food that other towns sent. That's why I say that for some it was a "business."

"They asked us for help."

After the earthquake, the construction workers decided to strike because their working conditions were very bad and their wages were very low. A contract was signed between management and labour, and it was recognized by the Ministry of Labour, which establishes workers' salaries. This collective contract took thirteen years—or eleven, I can't remember exactly—to be reached. These workers' wages hadn't been raised in all that time and the cost of living had gone up disproportionately.

Also, after the earthquake, the government imposed a labour law establishing a working day of twelve hours. That is, the workers had to work longer hours and on the other hand the price of the people's basic food, corn and beans, went up . . . Transportation costs rose as well. The worker found himself without a home, in a very difficult situation, and under frightful psychological pressure . . .

So a strike was started in a work center, in a place where some building was going on. The workers went to the University and stated their problem. At first there were about five hundred or eight hundred workers. They asked us for help. The form our help took initially was printing their document declaring that they were going out on strike and asking for the solidarity of other construction workers.

The next day more than half of all construction came to a halt. In addition to printing this document, we organized a few teams to take charge of distributing this material, as it was difficult for the workers to move from one center to another because they could be more easily detected by the police. The first measure the police took was to place guards around the construction sites. The following day the strike was almost total. And in three or four more days all construction work had stopped.

The construction workers had no place to meet, because the earthquake had demolished the union hall. A place at the University was given to them where they held their daily assemblies. A Strike Steering Committee was formed and work commissions were set up. Some made up and printed propaganda and gave information to the newspapers and radio, others visited the work centers and construction classes to build support for the strike and keep the workers informed. Every day one or two thousand construction workers met in the University, the situation was discussed and these people then moved to the classrooms where the other workers on strike were making plans.

The government responded with strong repression, and both workers and students were put in prison. Nevertheless, after nearly a month of the strike, the government—or the Committee, as there was really no government at that point, only an Emergency Committee headed by Somoza himself—was obliged to suspend the twelve hour day they'd imposed.

It's interesting to see how in that strike, for example, the newspaper *La Prensa* at first downplayed the event, and how a person had to urge the paper and go to its offices to have some things published. The Chamorro family has interests in construction but they couldn't deny the evidence, and in the long run . . .

Then shortly after there was another strike by the construction workers. The workers had already reconditioned a place where the CGT—the General Work Center—was, but this was leveled by the Guard. So then the workers had to resort to one of the neighbourhoods, to a neighbourhood church, and they met there. The Guard interfered and flattened the church. They were invited to the University again.

In reprisal Somoza threatened the University. He said that anyone in an organization or autonomous entity that lent assistance to the construction workers would be supervised. We saw that it wasn't wise for the workers to meet in massive public assemblies because the Guard would be constantly acting and they weren't going to let the strike develop. The only thing to be gained would be a greater number of workers and students thrown into jail.

The need to direct the strike in secret was put forward. There was one representative from the student movement on the construction workers' Strike Committee. The University Center did studies on the profits of the construction companies. We got our information from the engineering students who worked in the companies as assistants to the engineers and from an engineer connected with the University who worked with those companies.

The student movement in Nicaragua attempted to put itself at the service of the working class, the working class and the peasants. It put the intellectual capacity of its members at the service of the revolution. Of course as the students graduated, the proportion lessened but there were cases where professional women and men, either openly or in secret, worked through the student movement, or the Front itself, putting their knowledge and ability at the service of the people, knowing that it is the working class in alliance with the peasants that's going to lead the revolution in our country.

" . . . it's hard to make patients in need of attention understand why they're not going to get any."

In addition to the construction strikes through 1973 and 1974, there were also two very big strikes in the hospitals, lasting more than a month.

The hospital sector is very militant with women taking a great part in the struggles. The nurses in Nicaragua have to work many, many hours which can of course seriously affect their work. A woman who has worked for more than ten or twelve hours can't be of any help, and this can have very serious consequences for the sick person. In the first hospital strike, the nurses, besides asking for a higher salary and better working conditions, demanded better attention for the patients because the health problem is a problem often overlooked. The nurses accused the hospitals of giving the charity patients the medicines the hospitals happened to have on hand, or that were cheapest, instead of the ones they needed. The strike denounced the bad food, the poor attention given the patients and at the same time demanded better working conditions. They also denounced the businesses that some hospital authorities, partisans of the regime, were carrying on. The result was that some gains were made.

Later on there was another strike, also by the hospital sector, which covered national problems as well. Work stopped in all the hospitals. This kind of strike is very delicate because it can be a double-edged sword. These strikes can be utilized by the enemy to ruin the reputation of the doctor or the nurse who goes out, because it's hard to make patients in need of attention understand why they're not going to get any. The doctor comrades and the nurse comrades did give emergency service, but at a certain stage of the strike these doctors and nurses were ousted from the hospital. The comrades held meetings at the University and decided to organize people's clinics.

We worked with them to install these clinics with the help of the neighbourhood organizations. The University medical students, together with the doctors, lent their services. In these clinics people get medicines the hospitals don't give them. Sometimes there are even patients who can't be moved to the clinics and who are attended to in their homes by the comrades. In this way the population receives better attention than in the hospitals, where the patient first must have enough money before she or he has the "right" to attention. I believe that Nicaragua is the only country where health care, supposedly free to the public, actually has to be paid for. Not much money, but for the Nicaraguan it's a lot.

Talks on environmental health are offered in the neighbourhoods. The people are told why it's practically impossible for the doctor to do anything with the patients' health problems. Most of the time, when children come with diarrhea or vomiting or skin infections, these are a result of the environment, of the lack of latrines. The neighbourhood residents were made to see that as long as this system existed, the most the doctor could do was to give an aspirin for the pain or some medicine to stop diarrhea, but that the anti-diarrhea treatment couldn't do any lasting good because the child had to keep on living in the same house, eating the same food he was eating, without even the least hygiene in its preparation. In other words, those houses were sources of infection. It was a question of making the people aware.

Some work was done with the medical students and with the recent graduates, some of whom were doing their internship, to encourage reform of the medical studies' plan being contemplated within the general university reform plan. I said that the study plan of the Medical School in Nicaragua was strongly influenced by North American pharmaceutical companies through their donations. In one of the strikes, in a takeover of a building, we checked some archives and discovered that a North American pharmaceutical house had given a donation to the School of Medicine with the commitment of being able to direct the medical study plan in a certain direction. We denounced this. The doctors already graduated gave us great help in this because they could explain to the medical students how they were being used; how the doctor was being changed into a totally dehumanized person; how medicine, a highly humanitarian profession, was becoming completely commercialized; how they weren't taught to prevent sicknesses, only to cure them, and how the doctors weren't really concerned with preventing diseases because their salaries depended on the people being sick.

They explained the demands that medical doctors specialize and not be simply a general practitioner. In another system, in another kind of society, this is a very positive thing because it's assumed that the specialist has better qualifications and more skill. But in a country where the specialist earns up to a hundred *cordobas* a consultation, and more; where specialists have access only to the highest stratum of the population—since not even the middle classes can afford a specialist—then this doctor is being shaped not to satisfy the needs of the Nicaraguan people, but to satisfy the needs and whims of the bourgeois ladies who can indulge in the luxury of even inventing psychological illnesses and constantly visiting psychiatrists, psychologists, and all kinds of specialists. In reality this doctor is being shaped to satisfy the needs of North American imperialism.

The Nicaraguan doctor knows that the one who remains a general practitioner finds himself in the most remote places where there's no possibility of advancement. In his years in medical school the medical student is taught that the specialist acquires a certain status, a certain place, a certain social position, but that the general practitioner works in a very bad clinic with few medical techniques, and with a clientele that can't enable him to buy a car or a television set or a good house.

"PLAN YOUR FAMILY . . ."

There's a problem in Nicaragua—as in all of Latin America—one more manifestation of imperialist penetration in our countries: the implantation in the country of North American programs of population control which, on a continental scale, take on the proportions of genocide.

These programs reflect the point of view of a North American president, Johnson, who said that it costs less to kill a guerrilla before he or she is born. It's one way of trying to control the working class and the peasant class, the moving forces of revolution.

In Nicaragua there's a group called "Friends of the Americas." In this program young North Americans, knowingly or not, are detailed to carry out innoculation campaigns. The object used for innoculating is called a "peace pistol," a new system of vaccination, a kind of gun that does the job very quickly. It's a way of sterilizing adults as well as children. Men and women.*

This has been intensified since the earthquake, although even before there were placards that said: PLAN YOUR FAMILY, PRACTICE BIRTH CONTROL, RESPONSIBLE PARENTHOOD, that dealt with a series of issues that seemed to be innocent and even "beneficial" to the population. They said, for example, that responsible parenthood consists in having the children you can support, that nobody has a right to bring a child into the world if you can't support it. These campaigns didn't say that responsible parenthood consists in having the children the system allows you to support.

It's true that a woman loaded down with ten or twelve children isn't good but this birth control is a control imposed by the system. And imposed on one class specifically. It isn't a conscious question of the intellectual or material needs of the man or woman, but a control imposed by the system itself for the purpose of avoiding a demographic explosion which, after all is said and done, is going to hurt the system.

As the population increases, the exploited classes grow and unemployment is greater. That is, the source of the system's disintegration develops more, and the problems the government, the regime itself, can't face right now become more difficult to mitigate. They don't want things out of hand. This is the objective of the campaign, and this is what they don't tell you.

It's hard to attack this problem, it's hard to carry on a popular campaign against this work because they come to innoculate against polio, against measles—activities that can really be classified as philánthropic. But there are experiments—I think they were denounced in Colombia and El Salvador, also recently in Costa Rica—where they've sterilized people by means of a vaccine. And nobody guarantees they're innoculating against measles and nobody guarantees they're innoculating against polio. This has been denounced, especially lately. In early 1975,

---

* San Jose, Costa Rica, July 9, 1975 Prensa Latina (PL): In San Jose, Costa Rica, the fathers of Nicaragua refuse to have their children innoculated with vaccines from the United States, in view of accusations that they are also sterilizing agents . . . Vaccines against measles produced by Merke, Sharp and Dome and Connaugh against polio are applied in Nicaragua by members of the program "Friends of the Americas."

the Nicaraguan radios pointed out that some children who had received their three shots against polio were coming down with that disease. Probably those children did not receive anti-polio shots, but may have been sterilized.

As I said, it's hard to make people aware of this because sometimes you can't even show the real intention till a lot of harm has been done. An American group came, the "Peace Corps," and installed themselves in a certain neighbourhood. And they set up a clinic—they have the means to set up a clinic with specialists. The government isn't interested in solving, or the system can't solve, the health problems of the marginal population. This clinic was set up to solve these people's problems. And at times this surprises people; yet the Nicaraguan is characterized by his distrust of the *gringo* who shows up wanting to give him something. This is an element that permits the organizations of the left, the progressive sectors, to explain to the population these people's true intentions.

It's monstrous: I believe that in El Salvador each peasant, man or woman, who comes to be sterilized—and in this case it's a "voluntary" sterilization—is given a transistor radio. It's somewhat gross. It's the cheapest kind of propaganda. I don't know if they'll reach this point in my country.

These same organizations have brought the country many elements of social disintegration, like drugs. Through these organizations, imperialism succeeds in introducing elements that are totally corrupt and has made the use of drugs possible at almost massive levels among large sections of the youth. Undoubtedly drugs and other vices are found mainly in the middle classes and the high bourgeoisie, but these people are also able to penetrate sections of the young proletarians or the petty bourgeoisie, the lowest middle classes of the population.

I know of one "Peace Corps" group in the Matagalpa region that cultivated marijuana around the shores of the Rio Grande de Matagalpa. In Managua, in Colonia Centroamerica, there was a group of these young North Americans selling marijuana. And these people were able to bring in drugs that were unknown in the country, drugs like LSD, and a whole string of narcotics that had never beeen seen before.

It's grotesque to see how the middle and high bourgeoisie

imitate foreign customs—European and North American—and
how "playboys" increase, coming from England and from the
United States. The Yankees come to the country dressed like
"hippies" and look ridiculous besides the worker and the
young people of proletarian background.

In the University itself you can tell by the clothes if a person is
from the upper classes or the middle classes or the proletariat.
Proletarian young boys and those of the middle classes go around
in straight pants, not bell bottoms, and they don't wear platform
shoes or have long hair, and the young women don't wear long
skirts down to the ground. This kind of dress isn't Nicaraguan. It's
something you notice. The young men and women of the working
class dress modestly, and the men wear their hair short. The true
proletarian, the true Nicaraguan, isn't affected so easily by
European and North American culture.

"The Subtiavan Indian is always armed."

The native community of Subtiava is representative of the
struggle in the popular sectors of the Nicaraguan people. These
people live in the western part of the country, in Leon. They own
land. They were the original inhabitants of this region when the
Spanish colonists founded the city of Leon. It was a very important
community for its economic activity, in the country's life before
colonization—and they're a people with an enormous tradition of
struggle. In 1671 or 1681, in 1775 and later, the Subtiava Indians
rose up against the colony and carried out insurrections.

Their main means of living, then, was the land, and the problem
they've always had—and mobilized for—is the land. When the
colony came, they were deprived of their lands, but they kept some
tracts and got titles of ownership from the crown. The're still
keeping the titles of ownership.

As the cultivation of cotton has been widening in the country,
the Subtiavans have been pushed aside more and more. Their
lands have been snatched away. The Subtiava people are still
organized. They have their Community Council with a president.
Their main struggle has to do with the land the big landowners
took away from them.

They work as craftsmen and day labourers, and the women as domestics, in the city of Leon. Subtiava has practically become a district of Leon. To get together, to convene their meetings, the Subtiavans make use of the drum. The Subtiava drum. They still preserve the sounds. When they beat the drum the Subtiavan Indian knows when and where the meeting will be or if they are calling to make wire pikes.

They're constantly making pikes from the wire the big landowners spread to rob them of pieces of their property. The Subtiavan Indians go and make pikes and stretch the fence where it should be. They confront the Guard, armed with rifles and pistols and machetes—whatever they happen to have. The Subtiavan Indian is always armed. There are 15,000 of them.

One of the latest struggles was in 1974. The Subtiavans called a meeting where they decided to evict someone who had come and settled on their land. This man and his family weren't Subtiavans. It was a middle class not a bourgeois family but the Subtiavans claimed they couldn't allow this kind of thing because to allow anyone to settle on their land was a matter of principle. So they notified this person to leave. The person refused and was then ousted by the people.

They threw out that family, so the police intervened. It wasn't so easy for the police to enter the Subtiavan district. The police patrols coming into Subtiava had to enter very carefully. The Community Council, an almost military organization, had to go into hiding. It was protected by the people living there.

Because the Council was in hiding, the drums were left in the hands of the women. The press published a picture of the Subtiavan women with their drums. It was amazing to see, for example, how the Subtiavans working in Leon would, as soon as they heard the drum, leave their work right away and go to the place the drum was calling them to.

In that struggle there were demonstrations all the way to the middle of the city, protesting the big landowners and the Guard that had made their way into the district. Then there was a law suit against the Community Council and against its chief, comrade Mangus Verbis. But the Guard couldn't put this comrade in jail because he was protected by all the Subtiavans. And as I said, the Subtiavans always went around armed.

He came, gave his declarations, and said they weren't going to let anyone settle on their lands, and any time anyone took possession of Subtiavan lands, he'd be ousted. One of the conditions for getting Subtiavan land was that the buyer oppose Somoza. They took that condition very seriously: the Subtiavan who was a Somocist would be isolated inside his own community.

The Indians of Subtiava participated very actively in the campaigns for political prisoners, when there was a very extensive campaign to free comrade Francisco Ramirez, for example. He was the guard who had to spend five years in prison because he had handed over his rifle to the Sandinist Front. The Indians were present whenever there were charges against the Sandinist prisoners. They were present at the trial and beat their drums. When the University was under siege or when the Guard suppressed University activities, they were there immediately with the drum. The Guard was really afraid to face these Subtiavan peasants; the Subtiavan Indian is very combative, very determined.

In the last big campaign to free the political prisoners who had spent four and seven years in jail, the participation of the Subtiavans was very important: they not only came armed, but they also brought *la Gigantona*. Besides their drums . . .

La Gigantona is a form of expression of the Nicaraguan people. It's a huge effigy accompanied by a dwarf called Pepe. *La Gigantona* dances to the sound of drums, and the dwarf dances around her and recites ballads.

On that occasion the Subtiavans brought their *Gigantona*. Every neighbourhood, every native community has its official *Gigantona*. So they brought it and the verses Pepe recited were political, alluding to the oppression the Nicaraguan people live under, alluding to the Sandinist Front struggle and the problem of the prisoners.

The Subtiavans and their *Gigantona* also visited the homes of the principal Somicists and landowners. And there, with the *Gigantona* dancing and Pepe's poems, they accused those people.

The other political sectors, that is, the other political organizations of the country, didn't participate. This struggle was a struggle of the Front, headed by the Front. The people mobilized around the problem of the prisoners and denounced the general situation of the country. No other political party or any other political group actively participated.

The opposing bourgeoisie tried to take advantage of this movement. They had the nerve to offer to publicize the whole campaign, and to do it for free, in exchange for support for the bourgeois opposition movement. Both the people and the students rejected their proposition and went on with the campaign.

Of course the bourgeois newspapers opposed to Somoza had to publish some issues although they tried by every means within their reach to minimize the importance of what was going on. They de-emphasized the people's mobilization and how the people were responding to the Organization's call. Through this campaign the Organization came out strengthened. The troubled sectors were strengthened and besides, there were breaches opened in other sectors.

" . . . we suffered a very hard blow . . ."

In September 1973, we suffered a very hard blow in the life of the Organization—hard for me personally as well as for the organization.

On the night of September 17, my comrade and comrade Oscar Turcios—both members of the national administration—moved to a hideout in the village of Nandaime. A little while after leaving the house they were ambushed by the Guard. They were taken prisoner.

The next day, very early, Security ordered a Guard squad to the house they'd left. This squad was destroyed by the other occupants. They were two men comrades and two women comrades. Comrade Juan Jose Quesada and Jonathan Gonzales; I can't divulge the names of the two women.

After annihilating the squad the comrades abandoned the house. The comrades didn't know till that moment that Oscar and Ricardo Morales had been ambushed and arrested. The comrades went into the countryside. The Guard went after them. They divided into two groups, the two women succeeded in getting out of the place and deceiving the Guard, but the two men were surrounded and attacked by small planes. After several hours of fighting, the two men were assassinated.

Meanwhile, Oscar Turcios and Ricardo Morales were tortured and killed by Security. According to our information, comrade Oscar Turcios had an enormous quantity of bullet holes all over his body, in the back and especially in the chest. He was mutilated too, probably before he died, as a torture.

My comrade was shot mainly in the hands, and I believe his chest had eighteen bullet holes in it, and he'd been shot in the legs. Later the bodies were handed over, and they said the men had been taken out by a patrol for the purpose of tracking down the two women who had been able to escape, that at a bend in the road the men had tried to escape and the patrol had to fire. But the shots gave the lie to that, and so did the enormous number of blows—the fractures and mutilations both had suffered. This patrol was commanded by Orlando Hislop, the individual who interrogated me.

It wasn't the first crime committed in the offices of Security. There was the case of a student in Leon in 1967, comrade Rene Carrion. It was made to appear he'd committed suicide in the Office of Security. When the body was handed over there were still signs of the hands and feet having been tied and they said he was able to get hold of a gun and commit suicide.

There were the cases of comrades Casimiro Sotelo and others who were captured alive and assassinated. Comrade Denis Enrique Romero Zamoran was assassinated by National Security in 1972. This comrade was tortured so savagely that there wasn't a bone in his body that wasn't fractured and they made it look like an accident. They said they were taking him to prison in a vehicle and that he had jumped out—an impossibility because the Security cars are locked tight and no prisoners are ever taken in them unless their hands and feet are bound.

Comrade Romero Zamoran's body was totally destroyed and the clothes he wore weren't even soiled. He was tortured naked. He had fractures and sores all over his body, and his clothes weren't even dirty. When someone falls off a vehicle, the clothes are torn before the skin is damaged.

The same thing happened with comrades Oscar Turcios and Ricardo Morales.

When this happened, I was only two and a half months pregnant with the girl . . .

" . . . grabbed the guy by the throat and said to him: 'What the hell do you want?' . . ."

I remember some things Oscar Turcios and I did together. In 1961, while serving in Socialist Youth, we were entrusted by our cell to pass out leaflets in various parts of the capital. Comrade Turcios coordinated this and every member of the cell was assigned to a work area.

After distributing the leaflets we had a meeting place that was the control point where, at a prearranged time, we would meet to verify that we'd done our work and whether we'd had some mishap or if everything had turned out well and if we'd been able to carry out our work without being apprehended by the Guard.

We had a time limit to pass out the leaflets. It was a leaflet about May First, 1961. When I arrived at the corner of Ferreteria Lang and Avenida Bolivar nobody had come yet. It was two or three minutes before the appointed time. While there I noticed that a car had parked with only one person in it, a very elegant person, a man, the driver, dressed in white. I noticed that the car had a medical license plate on it.

This fellow parked the car and saw me and shut off the engine and got out. I didn't move from the spot, stayed there as if I didn't know what was happening. This doctor came over to where I was and with a rather engaging voice said hello. I didn't answer, turned around and started walking on the avenue. Then the fellow walked behind me. I walked faster and so did he. I turned into a street and came near a post where there was a guard, but I didn't dare talk to him since I didn't know if this guy following me was a member of Security, and then I'd be helping him in his work.

I walked very quickly, almost running, and tried to reach the control point. The man kept following me. The whole way the guy was telling me not to run, inviting me for a beer, to go someplace. When I was near the control point, I realized that nobody was there yet. Then I thought I'd have to take a taxi and get away, but it was almost midnight and at that hour there wasn't much traffic in that part of the city.

When I did reach the control point again I was going to go right on, but I noticed there was a shadow, and I was afraid because I thought it might be someone with the man who was chasing me. Nevertheless, when the guy reached that place the shadow threw himself on him and grabbed him by the throat. Then I realized it was comrade Turcios.

He grabbed the guy by the throat and said to him: "What the hell do you want?" and asked him why he was following me. The guy told him it was nothing; he was frightened, got into his car and drove off. I asked Oscar why he had done that; he didn't know if the man was from Security, or had a gun, or could have done something to him. But Oscar told me he couldn't contain himself. That was how Oscar was.

He was an impulsive comrade and in spite of being very calm when he had to work, when he saw another male or female comrade in trouble, it was hard for him to control himself. And it didn't matter if he ran a risk in helping us.

Oscar had a very jovial character. He was always singing and cracking jokes. He was a very generous person; it didn't matter to him if he sacrificed his well-being to help others.

He liked to participate in all the activities that were necessary, and when he did, he put his whole heart and soul into them. Without any doubt, Oscar came to be the center of any activity he was part of. He was known for that. In any place or activity or action he took part in, he was right in the middle of it.

He was a comrade with great sensitivity, sometimes concealing it with violent phrases. It made him very happy to take part in the May First demonstration.

Afterward, in 1966, the first of May 1966, Oscar took part and spoke in the House of the Worker, as a member of the Sandinist Front. I remember toward that day, Oscar was going around with increasing joy, singing all the time. He told me he had a surprise for all of us.

Around April 29 or 30 he told me to accompany him to where he was going to bring the surprise. He didn't yet let me know what the surprise was. I saw—yes—that he was carrying a very big bundle. On May 1 he and his friend Daniel Ortega told us what the surprise was—a huge gorilla effigy, almost as large as a man, dressed in a military uniform: it was a gorilla representing Somoza.

We carried this gorilla in the May First demonstration. It had a band around its chest representing the United States flag. Near the House of the Worker the gorilla was set on fire and burned. That's a sign of repudiation used a great deal by the townspeople. Even in their religious festivities they make an effigy of Judas, hang him and then set fire to it. We used that same method to repudiate Somoza. Oscar was following the tradition of the people.

After that May first Oscar gave me some flags of the Front that had been taken to the demonstration, and some FER flags to be put away. Later I had to leave the country and I returned near the end of the year, about October or November, just before going to the mountains to join the guerrilla group of Pancasan, in 1967.

"One of the last acts . . . and maybe the most important . . ."

One of the last acts of the Sandinist Front, and maybe the most important in those last days, was the act of December 27, 1974. It was the kidnapping of several servants of the dictatorship who were in Jose Maria Castillo's residence at a reception for the United States ambassador. It was a political act rather than a military one and dealt a direct blow to the Somoza dictatorship.

It's important to make an analysis of the living conditions in the country from at least 1970 or 1971 to 1974 to understand why the Sandinist Front had to resort to those methods to free the imprisoned comrades.

First, the Front originated around 1962 and had its first guerrilla experience at Bocay in 1963. Later we had Fila Grande and Pancasan in 1967. I told you about this before. On these two occasions we suffered partial failures that nevertheless provided us with an enormous and valuable experience regarding methods and forms of organization.

To understand why we failed, you have to bear in mind that in those years our revolutionary movement was just taking its first steps—there's enormous backwardness, ideological rather than political, in the country, which undoubtedly leads to blunders and at times to not being able to exactly channel the Nicaraguan people's eagerness for freedom.

Yet after these two actions, the Sandinist Front had accumulated enough experience to be able to carry the struggle forward and change itself into a real vanguard. That's how, after the years from 1970—exactly 1970—to 1974 when this action was taken, the Front went through a stage of accumulation and preparation of its forces.

It was a time when the Organization tackled the problem of avoiding the frontal response to the aggressive acts the regime was committing. On the other hand, the rightist forces as well as the Office of Security, which were interested in knowing what the Front was doing and where it was, provoked us on numerous occasions. It provoked us often: assassinating comrades, threatening to assassinate the Sandinist prisoners who were in the Model prison—in short, countless provocations intending to make the Front respond somewhere.

It was hard to have to use restraint, to be unable to respond openly to these provocations. We were also passing through a very hard stage because we had to look for resources without being able to use the name of the Front directly. Nevertheless we found some support, we found contributors, and the Organization developed to such an extent that it was capable of dealing a blow to the regime on December 27.

That blow, the kidnapping of those people who were in Jose Maria Castillo's house at a reception for the United States ambassador, had as an objective the freeing of the comrades who were in prison—some since 1967—and also the obtaining of funds, although the main objective was the freedom of the comrades, denouncing repression in the country, demanding salary raises for the exploited and oppressed workers, and at the same time actually getting the money demanded.

All the demands stated by the Organization were complied with. Commando Juan Jose Quezada's messages were published as demanded and in the form required. Fourteen comrades were set free. And the government gave, or at least announced it would give, salary raises to the exploited sectors and also to the common guards of the National Guard.

To illustrate a little of the repression being imposed on the countryside . . . and not only in the countryside but in all the cities, it's enough to mention a few examples.

In September 1973, the Guard assassinated four comrades: two members of the Administration—comrades Ricardo Morales and Oscar Turcios—and two members of the Organization—Juan Jose Quezada and Jonathan Gonzalez. Juan Jose Quezada was a fighter distinguished for his bravery. Previously, comrade Juan Jose Quezada had hijacked an airplane to Cuba, if I'm not mistaken, on November 4, 1970, commemorating the assassination of comrade Casimiro Sotelo.

In September 1973, twenty-three native leaders were persecuted by the Guard. These were leaders of the Subtiava community who were reclaiming their land. And in November 1973 there was a strike of the Licorera Nacional workers, also broken up by the Guard. In December of that same year the campaign to free comrade Francisco Ramirez Urbina and the Salvadoran Efrain Nortlewalton was organized. In this campaign thirty-five leaders were arrested and tortured.

In 1974 the repression in the countryside increased; using as a pretext the kidnapping of a Somocist lieutenant by an armed group of peasants. The Guard sent out its squads and assassinated hundreds of families. And in 1974 the helicopters appeared again. Helicopters flying over the mountains of Nicaragua bring terror, because the peasants who are taken prisoner are lifted up by them and then let fall from high altitudes, and when they hit the ground they're completely smashed to pieces.

In February 1974, they assassinated comrade Manuel Aviles, in Rivas. In April they killed comrade Ramon Gonzales. In the west the peasant population regained lands that had been taken over by officers of the Guard, lands in Palo Alto and Palo Grande. This time the repression against the peasants was under the command of Colonel Gonzalo Evertz. At that time they put forty-eight entire families in jail, old people and children . . . and the five peasants the Guard accused of directing that group "disappeared" . . .

There were numerous cases of massive rapes: women stripped and hooded and dragged naked through the various districts. Women of the Hernandez family in 1971, the Flores women in 1973, and the Castil sisters in 1974.

In May of 1974 they arrested several peasants, among them Luis Garcia Cardenal, and twenty-six others—women and children. We saw names like Maria Felicia de Garcia who was arrested with her seven month old son. Like Abelina Munoz de Martinez with four children. And many others . . .

Comrade Alfredo Medina was also assassinated, and Andres Lopez, Miguel Angel Pos and Jose Montenegro were tortured. They accused these comrades of being cattle thieves and of having arms hidden in their houses. The accusation of cattle thief is very common to justify repression in the countryside. They say they go looking for cattle thieves, *matavacas*, and this gives them the excuse to use indiscriminate repression. They kill old people, women and children under this pretext of looking for cattle thieves . . .

In New Guinea—this is a peasant colony, or more accurately, a concentration camp, in the west where they take peasants who've been robbed of their lands in other places—New Guinea, then, is where they oppressed and imprisoned Teresa de Leon Perez. This was done on the orders of Cornelio Hueck, a servant of the Somoza regime for many years, a man always distinguished for his loyalty to the Somoza family. He is the same man who sold the INVA lands that day. Their objective this time was to take that comrade's lands away from her.

All through 1974, there was as much repression in the cities as in the countryside. They captured student leaders, among them the president of the CUN, who while travelling to Venezuela and Panama had denounced the situation he was living in.

All through that year repression increased. This was also the case for the arrested comrades. For many years there had been campaigns to free the prisoners. Mothers joined a committee with some honest intellectuals, with the student movement. Every year there was a campaign, an appeal before the Supreme Court of Justice; a denunciation of the prisoner situation was taken before the Senate and the House of Deputies, and these institutions were made to see that those prisoners were being tried under false accusations, and that many had served their terms, as in the case of comrades Daniel Ortega and Jacinto Suarez.

"December came and there were no plans to free the comrades . . ."

In 1974 the country had a new constitution, drawn up by the Constituent Assembly. This Constituent Assembly was a product of the Aguero-Somoza pact, a Constituent Assembly convened for the sole purpose of engineering the reelection of Somoza while making sure it didn't appear manipulated. They changed various regulations and made it look as if Somoza were a new candidate after a period in which he hadn't governed. But the truth is—apart from the fact that the Government Council was controlled by the Liberal Party—after the 1972 earthquake, a few months after the Council was formed, Somoza himself was appointed president of the National Committee of Emergency, and it was really he who directed and controlled the entire political and economic activity of the country.

Nevertheless this new Constitution left a loophole. In their eagerness to get it over with quickly so that Somoza could once again take up the reins of government sooner—formally—they left a loophole through which it could be demanded that the prisoners be released. The Constitution didn't call for conviction for one of the crimes the prisoners were being accused of. On that basis a new campaign was started. But they convened the Constituent Assembly again and repaired this error.

December came and there were no plans to free the comrades, Somoza had been formally elected again, there was enormous repression, there were many prisoners, and besides . . . the Organization was aware that by legal means, by peaceful means, the government was never going to release these prisoners. And as repression increased, it was becoming more and more difficult for the Organization to keep silent. On the other hand, as I told you, the Organization had been gathering strength throughout this period and was capable of responding to the situation.

As soon as a meeting of the urban and mountain resistance command was held, where the situation was anlaysed, the pros and cons seen, the Organization's fighting ability evaluated, the body of troops they could count on known, it was decided to carry out an armed action that would deal a heavy blow to the dictatorship, that would "checkmate" it.

After this meeting the action was planned in all its details, and the various information teams began to work: intensive preparation was provided to the selected teams. The participating comrades were prepared, not only by being given military training but by political instruction as well. These commandos spent several days in their barracks, ready to go out and fight.

The day of the action at Jose Maria Castillo's residence, they had to face some twelve or fourteen agents. The fight was fast. In spite of the resistance put up by the system's cops, the attack went so quickly that they didn't have time to recover from their surprise. There were about eight casualties—killed and wounded—among the servants of the dictatorship. On our part, one comrade was slightly wounded.

A short while after we got inside the house the Guard came, and in spite of the fact that there were people inside, they attacked with hand grenades. The hostages were terrified and hurled curses against Somoza, against the Guard, and against the whole government. They fought amongst themselves accusing each other of collaborating with the government.

It was decided to send one woman, a hostage, to explain the terms of the commandos' demands. The servants and musicians were freed, as were the women.

Somoza tried to establish direct communication with the commandos. They refused on principle to set up direct communication with anyone from the government, and demanded that negotiations be carried out through an intermediary recognized for his honesty. Archbishop Monsignor Obando y Bravo was chosen.

This action demonstrated the political, moral, and military ability of the Organization. The regime now understood the quality of the enemy it was facing. The Sandinist Front had taken a qualitative step compared with previous years.

"Three women comrades took part in this action."

Three women comrades took part in this action. The military action. Of course data on preparing the action and obtaining information can't be given, but I'm absolutely sure there were many women involved.

The women comrades who fought in this action had different backgrounds. They answer to numbers two, eight and fifteen. Comrade number two is the daughter of a Nicaraguan worker who, because of the conditions in his country, felt obliged to go into exile where he stayed for a long time. His daughter is an example of the attitude Nicaraguans preserve in exile. She returned to the country while still young and could see the outrages the Guard committed against the people. In a country near to Nicaragua she became a revolutionary fighter.

Already in 1968 this comrade was participating in actions denouncing Lyndon B. Johnson's visit, Johnson's tour in 1968. In 1970 this woman joined a professional body of troops in the Organization, and left her university studies. In hiding she worked to train other women from the most exploited, the most oppressed sectors who had had little possibility of being educated. She said that experience was filled with many good memories and at no time will she forget the comrades who worked beside her. She also has good memories of the solidarity of the women from the districts where she worked. There were cases where women comrades refused to eat in order that the professional clandestine teams could eat.

In the Los Robles fighting, comrades number two, three, and twelve took part in securing one of the vehicles used to go to the mansion. Number two was the one charged with pointing a gun at the driver. She said she explained to him that it wasn't a robbery. When she stated this, the driver said: "Then it must be an action of the Sandinist Front for National Liberation."

She was carrying a short-barrelled carbine M-1, a Walter PK-32 pistol and a fragmentation grenade. When she went into the house she shouted: "Halt. Nobody move. This is an attack of the Sandinist Front."

She recounted how one of the hostages had told her that for him it was harder to manage women than men. He said that the women of the raiding expedition were more stubborn, stronger . . . And another of the hostages said he believed that the women commandos in this action were capable of surpassing the men—in energy.

Number eight, another of the women who took part, comes from a family of small businessmen, from the petty bourgeoisie. She has taken part in marches and meetings and anti-Somoza acts since she was very young. Her family belongs to the opposition. In 1970 this comrade became involved with the protest of the education workers. On that occasion she formed part of the group of young people who composed and sang popular slogans. In 1970 she participated in the massive movement of September condemning the ferocious Somocist repression and participated as well in the takeover of Christian churches all through the country. In 1972, while she was studying at the University, she worked in the student movement and was involved in the construction workers' struggle. She belonged to student groups who used singing as a weapon of struggle.

Afterward this comrade joined groups that carried out work in the lower class neighbourhoods. She could feel the oppression but also people's enthusiasm—the enthusiasm of the exploited—for the struggle. Comrade number eight said that she still hasn't forgotten the words of a little old woman who, in an act where there wasn't any order, said: "If this is the way we are, how are we going to wage the war?"

In the Los Robles fighting, she was in the group that did the final checking of the Castillo mansion to ensure that an operational situation existed. When they arrived to take over the mansion, she fired a .38 at the left flank. This comrade was also carrying a .22 to use in the defense of the place.

When the commando unit arrived, it found the front door locked. Number eight tried to open it by herself but she wasn't strong enough, and so, addressing the most muscular male comrade of the unit, she ordered: "Number eleven, the door!" Number eleven threw himself with all his strength against the door and opened it.

Once inside the house, number eight exclaimed: "Nobody move. This is the Sandinist Front."

Comrade fifteen came from the educational sector. From 1961 on she's been a member of the teachers' union. And has taken part in the lockouts of that period, demanding a raise in wages from the fifty-three dollars a month that workers earned in those days . . . She did practical work in the union. She committed herself to clandestine work at a very difficult time—just after the Sandinist Front experienced the cruel reverses of 1967 in the Fila Grande and Pancasan and in the city.

Since then she has been underground. She hasn't been captured in spite of the length of time she's been a militant and fighting in the underground. On January 15, 1970 she came close to being caught. That was the day Leonel Rugama and several other militants of the Sandinist Front were killed. At that time she was in an Organization local in a Managua district. She told us how the repressive forces were going through the district and how they casually ran into her and asked her if she had seen any suspicious-looking women.

She kept her cool and talked with the Guard troops without giving any sign that she was a clandestine fighter. She tried to get away saying that she had been on her way to a nearby store to buy a soft drink. But the patrol detained her and told her that no adult could walk around. Then she called a child and asked him to go and buy her the soft drink and gave him the empty soft drink bottle she was carrying. The Security men stopped paying attention to her because in doing what she did she showed them she was in no hurry to leave the place.

The militant women of the Sandinist Front did important work in the Los Robles action. These comrades in themselves synthesized the courage and ability of the militant women of the Front. They've had a great experience, an uninterrupted period of struggle, and have given proof of true self sacrifice.

There's a lot of data on these women, about their many valuable deeds—acts that characterize them as women of great humanitarian qualities—that can't be publicized for security reasons. I don't think it's necessary to give out a lot of information about these comrades. If they deserved the honour of being chosen as members of the "Juan Jose Quezada" commando unit, that in itself testifies to their quality.

"At this time the situation in the country . . . can be characterized politically and militarily as good . . ."

The action ended on December 31 with the accomplishment of

the planned objectives: freedom for the fourteen comrades, getting the money we asked for, publication of the messages—the "Juan Jose Quezada" commando messages as well as those that denounced the condition of the country. The demands for a salary raise for the common guards were also met and a raise in salaries was announced for the other exploited sectors. Our comrades left for Cuba on December 31—the commando unit and prisoners.

Two hours after the action "a state of siege and martial law" was declared. After the action had ended, the situation in the country was difficult. Repression was very intense. Cities in the north suffered enormous repression. During the day they made an effort to make things appear calm but at night there was a curfew and people couldn't go around after six in the evening without a safe conduct pass issued by the Guard. Several comrades and student leaders were arrested. The president of the University Center died as a result of beatings he received. Many women were arrested. An enomous number of peasants were imprisoned and killed in the concentration camps. The terror imposed by the regime was the result of their inability to keep hidden from the people the actions of the Front. They had to acknowledge their defeats. The Guard was impotent in the face of the Front.

This repression was made known throughout the world by international cable. The news agencies of imperialism couldn't deny the conditions existing in the country. The Organization circulated secretly throughout the country lists of those who had disappeared or been arrested, made known where figures were available the casualties suffered by the Guard . . . Of course the agencies didn't give any details, although they did recognize the existence of these clandestine news reports given out by the Organization to the Nicaraguan people.

At this time the situation in the country can be characterized politically and militarily as good. When a regime has to resort to violence that savage, it is an indication of their impotence to maintain the status quo and the "peace" that Somoza has given so much lip service to lately, and also gives some indication of the Organization's ability to defend itself. In spite of the repression, the Organization didn't suffer great casualties and no important center or group of the Front was struck down.

"To understand the reasons why sections of the bourgeoisie can adopt progressive positions, you must always bear in mind the characteristics of Somoza's dictatorship."

I said that the December 27 action was one of the most important, if not the most important action carried out by the Sandinist Front in recent times. It marked the start of a new stage: a stage that could be characterized as "open warfare" against the tyranny, against the system. The action was political rather than military, though it's true that the military skill of the FSLN was a very important factor in achieving success. But its objectives were political.

This action dealt a blow to the Somoza dictatorship and isolated it politically, internally as well as at the international level. On the national level, this was reflected by the fact that the dictator felt obligated to give in and had to forget his declarations that he'd never bow before the demands of the guerrillas if faced with a situation of this kind.

We received information that one sector that supported him put pressure on him to give in. It was evident even during the action when the hostages incriminated each other. There were those who called Somoza stupid or an imbecile when he didn't give in immediately or when he tried to surprise the Sandinist commandos by having the troops of the Guard approach the besieged residence.

After December 27 the active political forces polarized in a curious way. On the one hand there was a polarization in the bourgeoisie itself—the camps divided between the sector supporting the government and the opposition. This was because Somozas' dictatorship has been characterized by obstructing the participation of others in the country's economic life. A large sector of the bourgeoisie has been pushed aside and their control limited. This provides for the opposition to Somoza within the bourgeois sector.

On the other hand, within the opposition bourgeoisie there's divergence. There's a strong sector of the bourgeoisie that is progressive. Among those freed by the Juan Jose Quezada Commando Unit we find some comrades who collaborated with the Front. There was for example, Jaime Cuadra, who was president

of the Nicaraguan Coffee Growers' Cooperative. To understand
the reasons why sections of the bourgeoisie can adopt progressive
positions, you must always bear in mind the characteristics of
Somoza's dictatorship.

At the moment this bourgeois group lacks the right kind of
political leadership, and runs the risk of being absorbed by the
formal bourgeoisie on the other side. Therefore, one of the main
concerns of the Organization is to propitiate their political activity,
move them to be able to maintain an independent policy, making it
possible for a proper leadership to appear, and avoiding their
being controlled by the more reactionary sectors of the
conservative bourgeoisie.

On the international level, the actions of the dictatorship have
been condemned. For example, the magazine *Vision* reported in
the January 15, 1975 issue, that the FSLN commando action
showed "the ineffectiveness of certain authoritarian regimes that
combat it (the urban guerrilla movement)." Many Latin American
and European governments condemn the dictatorship. But the fact
that they condemn the dictatorship does not mean they've
supported the revolutionary movement. This is a very important
point since international solidarity is something that has a very
definite significance—is very important.

*"I think it would be interesting to try to make an assessment of the
political forces at work in the country . . ."*

I think it would be interesting to try to make an assessment of
the political forces at work in the country because of the influence
the FSLN action of December 27 has had on the activity and per-
spectives of these forces. The commando action not only marked
a new stage for the Organization, but it clearly charted a course, at
least for the immediate future, to continue the struggle to free the
country.

The country's political forces divide in the following manner:
Somoza's Liberal Party, now in power; the Traditionalist
Conservative Party; the bourgeois opposition grouped in the
Democratic Union of Liberation (UDEL); and the FSLN.

Let's look at Somoza's Liberal Party. It is a party in a state of disintegration, a *caudillo*, a one man party controlled by Tacho who counts on support from the United States Embassy, the National Guard, and one sector of the Conservative party to hold power. A sign of this disintegration is the breakdown of the part of the party controlled by Ramiro Sacasa, cousin of the Somozas, who has been called a constitutionalist and who is now formally opposing the Somozas within the UDEL.

The Traditionalist Conservative Party is also in a state of disintegration. For a long time this party was characterized by the tyranny of the Chamorro family. A tyranny that in a practical sense ended when Fernando Aguero ousted Pedro Joaquin Chamorro from its ranks. But Pedro Joaquin Chamorro heads a group called Conservative National Action. This group formally opposes the regime, also within the UDEL. Chamorro is a capitalist, editor of the newspaper *La Prensa*, a newspaper of the opposition but pro-imperialist.

The Traditionalist Conservative Party is very divided: in addition to Conservative National Action, we have two other big groups diverging over the question of supporting Somoza. They are headed by Fernando Aguero and Paguaga.

Fernando Aguero and his group made an agreement with Somoza and lent themselves to the clownish actions of the Constituent Assembly, which was nothing but a maneuver to guarantee the continuation of the Somoza family in power. And Paguaga is the conservative who displaced Aguero in supporting the Somozas after Aguero protested when, right after the earthquake, he felt even more pushed aside and deprived of his share of the national funds and the government's robbery of international aid.

The Independent Liberal Party is in the UDEL as well. The PLI originated in the years 1944 to 1947 as a result of a breaking apart of the Nationalist Liberal Party. It represents mainly the intellectual petty bourgeoisie—doctors, lawyers, some merchants or middle class contractors, and an occasional landowner. As I say, elements of the petty bourgeoisie.

In its beginnings the PLI had some social base which it's been losing, mainly because of the instability of the sector it represents and because of the inactivity that's required of the parties or political groups that have no part in government control. These parties frame their activities within the "legality" that the Somoza dictatorship allows or choose the kind of conspiracy that ends in a coup. Yet within the PLI you can find some honest and sincerely oppositional members of the petty bourgeoisie.

The Christian Social Party is another part of the UDEL. It has some social base within the petty bourgeoisie. Until 1969 its ranks had young people who took leadership roles in the student movement. These young people have been gradually abandoning its ranks, mainly because of the duality of this group's political positions. There are even some comrades in our Organization who some years ago were working with the PSC. You have to be careful with the Christian Social Party as it is not a very staunch ally. In the various times the oppositional bourgeoisie has tried to become allied, this party was the first to break the alliance. Like all the member groups of the UDEL, their principal concern has been to obtain a legal personality.

The Nicaraguan Socialist Party (Communist) also forms part of the UDEL. However, it doesn't control the UDEL. The bourgeoisie controls it in the person of Pedro Joaquin Chamorro.

The Sandinist Front for National Liberation has been shown to be the only organization that is presently prepared to head the struggle of the Nicaraguan people. The only organization capable not only of surviving in the state of repression Nicaragua lives in, but of developing, of growing in quality and numbers, of dealing political and military blows that really hit where it counts.

"Nicaragua is a country in crisis . . ."

It's important to understand what the UDEL represents in the present political situation. It could provide an easy way out of a difficult situation for North American imperialism. To understand this, it's important to know a bit about the policy imperialism is now wielding in the country.

Nicaragua is a country in crisis, not only economically but also politically. The crisis grows worse and worse. Confronted with this situation the various political forces see things differently and attempt different solutions.

North American imperialism, on its part, carries out a clearcut policy which up to now has been one of definite support for the Somoza dictatorship. You can be sure of this. It's known there are some 300 *gringo* officials—uniformed officials—in Nicaragua. And we know that behind every *gringo* official dressed in a uniform there are at least ten more North American agents in charge of information, logistics, etc. We also know of the presence of agents of the Brazilian regime in the northern zone. They are operative troops not military advisers. Just imagine: 300 military men in uniform—Yankees—in a city of 300,000 inhabitants like our capital Managua. Over 3000 foreign individuals in a small country of two million people, 3000 individuals directly interfering in the country. in the service of imperialism, supporting the Somoza dictatorship.

It's clear that for the present imperialism has made up its mind in favour of Somoza's repressive policy. This isn't capricious, imperialism is for Somoza because it guarantees the survival of the system, guarantees North American interests in the country. Imperialism isn't interested in Somoza because he's Somoza. It isn't interested in defending the dictatorship, or in defending the system as such. The moment Somoza fails to offer enough guarantees, at that moment the support will be taken away. And then the UDEL could be the card the *gringos* would play since the UDEL isn't planning the destruction of the system or even threatening it. The only thing it's planning is to rejuvenate it, apply new make-up.

". . . a long struggle, a prolonged popular war."

Bearing this situation in mind, that is, taking into account the country's conditions, our organization, the FSLN, is planning a long struggle, a prolonged popular war. The length of this war isn't a question to be determined by anybody's desire, it depends on internal conditions and in great measure on the relation of forces in the international camp.

When I told you that for us international solidarity has a very clear meaning, and that it's something of great importance from our point of view, I was thinking of the struggle of Sandino. For Sandino the lack of that solidarity, the isolation into which his struggle was forced, played a decisive role in his decisions subsequent to the departure of the forces intervening in the country.

We have to look at this carefully. Right now imperialism has another face, the face of the aggressor in Vietnam, of the kidnapper of Vietnamese children, of the CIA that carries out its actions everywhere; of a decadent monster in a serious economic and moral crisis. Besides, the relation of forces is different. Now there's a powerful socialist camp in the world.

At present, international solidarity for the FSLN translates concretely into isolation of the Somoza dictatorship at the world level. The attitude of other governments, of other nations, influences the attitude imperialism adopts toward the dictatorship. The FSLN needs international solidarity to strike and isolate the dictatorship. We're taking charge of dealing it a blow from the inside. We've shown our ability to do that.

We're planning a prolonged war, but we're not discarding the possibility of another maneuver by imperialism. What action it will take depends directly on its interests and will be influenced by the revolutionary movement as it develops and grows. It's important to see that any change, anything that happens, at the political level, is determined by the activity of the Front.

If imperialism believes that the repression or the repressive policies of Somoza can exterminate the revolutionary movement, then it will go on supporting Somoza and the repression. If it believes it can deal a blow to the Sandinist Front with certain reforms, certain changes in policy then it's going to permit, and even begin to promote the change. In other words, whatever option imperialism risks in the country, it's going to have to reckon with the presence of the Front.

If this sort of change doesn't take place, we're prepared. We have the capacity to confront whatever forms of repression are adopted. I'm convinced that with the continuation of the repressive policy, the only thing they'll accomplish is to increase the discontent, radicalize the people more and more, including the most honest, most progressive sectors of the bourgeoisie.

They can even intervene directly by way of the CONDECA or with its army, and we won't be annihilated because the people of Nicaragua recognize the Sandinist Front as their vanguard and because the Nicaraguan people have demonstrated that imperialism can be defeated in Nicaragua. The Sandinist struggle of the 1930s dealt the first defeat to imperialism in Latin America.

If policies do change, then of course things will be different. But we'll also be sure of not being defeated. We don't want to avoid change and we are sure that we can deepen it. Besides determining what kind of politics imperialism is playing in the country, we'll be able to radicalize it, carry forward the change to victory. But it's important to emphasize that in the objective situation at this time, no democratic opening appears imminent.

At present the Sandinist Front is determined to consolidate militarily. To a great extent this has been done. We're determined to achieve a greater political and organizational development, internally as well as externally. I believe we'll accomplish this as we ally ourselves with new sectors, as our ranks are strengthened with proletarian militants. We'll create a popular army, an army capable of confronting any enemy in the future, any interventionist force.

The situation in Nicaragua is somewhat different, or much different, than in any other country of Latin America. We have a revolutionary movement that relies on a unified leadership, a leadership that has known how to confront its own internal problems, bearing in mind that unity is a determining factor in carrying the struggle forward.

Besides, and this is very important, we are a growing revolutionary movement, a rising movement, one that it hasn't been possible to destroy, one that after each surge of repression has come out stronger—purifying itself along the way—without dividing into splinter groups. When a revolutionary movement is powerful, it can rise up again when it's struck down, and if, on the other hand, the imperialists try to isolate or exterminate it by "democratizing" the country, it's in a position to deepen, radicalize, and turn democratization in its favour.

" . . . all our people will dream in colour."

Casimiro. Julio. Ricardo. Maria Castil. Leonel. Luisa Amanda. So many others. In Nicaragua our yearnings for freedom are very great; the people have suffered too much.

Now I'm thinking about my childhood. About the countryside. About the peasant who died giving birth, who died of hunger. Of exploitation and misery.

I'm thinking about the women in jail, the peasant-prostitute, the worker-thief.

I'm thinking about my own mother and her unfinished struggle. About our fallen comrades and those who are still alive.

We'll keep on struggling. So someday all our people will dream in colour.

CHRONOLOGY OF INTERVENTION, REPRESSION AND STRUGGLE

Principal United States invasions of Nicaragua: 1853, 1854, 1857, 1894, 1898, 1899, 1910, 1912-25, 1926-33.

IMPOSITION OF TYRANNY [1926-1956]

1926-1933 According to official North American sources, in this period more than 5000 Nicaraguans died because of the war. The real figure is much higher. If we add Nicaraguans sacrificed in previous Yankee interventions, and the thousands killed under the Somoza terror in the decades after 1933, the number of victims resulting from North American intervention and domination in Nicaragua comes to not less than 100,000.

1934 In the course of political discussions, after the armed North American interventionists had been thrown out, Augusto Cesar Sandino was treacherously assassinated. Massive genocide against the peasants in the mountains.

1935 Failure of an uprising of National Guard (GN) elements, the government army, against the clique controlled by Anastasio Somoza Garcia.

1937 The Sandinist veteran Pedro Altamirano assassinated in the mountains.

1944 June: founding of the Nicaraguan Socialist Party (Communist). Group of rubber plantation workers take up arms against the Somoza regime.

1944-1947 Massive actions against Somoza by students and other popular sectors. In 1947 Somoza forbids the functioning of all unions.

1948-1956   Somocist repression increases further. Isolated elements carry out anti-government work. In 1948 armed action against the tyranny. The veteran Sandinist Juan Gregorio Colindres assassinated. In 1949 due to popular pressure, Somoza permits the formation of unions, but only if they "show loyalty" to him. In April 1954, an armed movement, whose political leadership is monopolized by bourgeois elements, fails. Among the participants assassinated is the shoemaker Optaciano Morazon, a veteran Sandinist.

RESURGENCE OF POPULAR RESISTANCE

1) The precursory years [1956-1961]

The years 1955-1961 were marked by serious intensification of imperialist domination of the Nicaraguan economy.

1956   Ascendancy of the world-wide struggle for national liberation is reflected in Nicaragua. For the first time since the period of Sandino, a representative sector of popular interests acts independently: young Rigoberto Lopez gives up his life assassinating the tyrant Somoza. At the same time a revolutonary student group appears and publishes two issues of *The University Student* on the presses of Edwin Castro, Rigoberto's friend, who is imprisoned and later assassinated. Right after Somoza's execution Luis Morales Palacio, Jorge Rivas Montes, Ramon Orozco, Bonifacio Miranda, Ausberto Narvaes, and Cornelio Silva are also assassinated.

1957   A group of army members conspire against the tyranny. Among them is Carlos Ulloa who dies in April 1961 fighting beside the Cuban people at Playa Giron. Victor Rivas Gomez and Napoleon Ubilla are assassinated by the regime in 1959 when they refuse to surrender to the forces of the tyranny. The conservative leadership that controlled the headquarters of the 1957 conspiracy is the cause of the failure. Nicaraguan women make use of suffrage for the first time.

1958   January: the military man, Victor Rivas Gomez, escapes from prison; months later, he hijacks one of Somoza's airplanes in Miami, Florida, to be used against the regime. April: on the Nicaraguan frontier near Cifuentes in Honduras, a meeting takes place between Nicaraguans resolved to take up arms against Somoza; they are persecuted by the Honduran authorities. Influence of the Cuban struggle: M-26-7 flags appear in different parts of the country; a dam in Rio Chiquito is baptized "26 of July." Parties opposed to Somoza demand electoral guarantees. Worker protests among waiters, drivers of vehicles, etc. May: government obliged to grant a certain autonomy to the University. July: massive student actions in Leon, seat of the National University, repudiating visit of the North American functionary Milton Eisenhower; Sandino's name is mentioned for the first time since his assassination. Strike of hospital workers. Various worker sectors threaten to strike August 1 for 2 per cent salary raise. Radio announcers organize union. Siuna y Neptuno Gold Mining Company miners protest not having received wages since September 1953. Somoza imposes radio censorship. August: wives and mothers of service men start radio campaign on behalf of six Air Force men condemned for political events of November 1957. Madam of a house of prostitution, Nicolasa Seville, organizes a fascist paramilitary group and begins to attack radio stations. October: in mountains of Yaule, veteran Sandinist Ramon Raudales, named head of last guerrilla detachment by Sandino 25 years earlier, falls in combat. Simultaneous massive student actions in Leon against tyranny's repression.

1959 February 21: University Center (CUUN), national students' organization, issues document commemorating assassination of Sandino. VIVA SANDINO slogans secretly painted on walls. First massive mobilization of urban youth sectors. June 24: Nicaraguan and Honduran army forces prepare and carry out massacre of Nicaraguan guerrillas on frontier location El Chaparral. July 23: in Leon, Somoza's repressive forces machine gun a peaceful students' march, leaving over a hundred dead and wounded. August-December: guerrilla actions in Peublo Nuevo, Chachagon, Yamla and Las Bayas.

1960 January: young prisoners accused of planting bombs at government establishments. Selim Schible and other young people arrested for burning officials' cars and sabotaging government installations. Guerrilla actions near Orosi, southern frontier point. February: guerrilla action in El Dorado, northern frontier point. Vehicle burnings of Somocist elements. Student strike in School of Agriculture. May: thousands of demonstrators stone building of official newspaper *Novedades* and exhibition hall *El Porvenir*, both controlled by Somozas. Some demonstrators confront the GN with fire arms on sidewalks of central market. May-August: several political prisoners assassinated; executioner Isaac Seville executed sometime later. Massive juvenile demonstrations bearing the red and black emblem. Julio Buitrago, Rigoberto Cruz and Casimiro Sotelo participate. July: crippled student Julio Oscar Romero assassinated by elements of National Security; 5000 persons attend funeral. Massive student street fights; burning of official vehicles and army jeep, stoning of GN, commemorating students sacrificed July 23. University Center (CUUN) denounces preparation in Nicaragua of imperialist armed aggression against Cuba. November: armed anti-Somocist action in Jinotepe and Diriamba. Eisenhower orders intervention in Nicaraguan waters of airplane carrier *Shangri-la*. Repression increases. Selim Schible, Edmundo Perez and several other rebels arrested in la Concha for revolutionary activities.

1961   January: student strike in School of Engineering. Dock workers threaten "sit down" strike. Strike of workers in graphic arts. March: Yankee invasion at Bay of Pigs. April: Selim Schible, Edmundo Perez and other youths are accused and imprisoned for revolutionary activity. Mercenary expedition against Cuba ("Happy Valley" in CIA code) leaves from Puerto Cabezas and is defeated at Playa Giron (Bay of Pigs). Physicians' strike in Matagalpa.

2) Fight of the Sandinist Front for National Liberation [1961-1974]

1961   July: a group of young Nicaraguan revolutionaries, supported by veteran Sandinist Santos Lopez and several others, constitute movement to be called   Sandinist Front for National Liberation (FSLN). August: organization of clandestine Sandinist elements in Managua. Massive action of transportation workers against rise in price of fuel. October: strikes of agronomy students.

1962   January: some young people accused of distributing "subversive" propaganda arrested. April: massive actions of teaching profession known as "Operation Justice." May: insurrectional organizational activity in Casa Colorada, near Managua. June: militants of the Sandinist Front intensify contact with mountainous area near Rio Coco. July: street protests, closing of streets, impromptu meetings, opposition to GN, arrests and beatings, burning of Yankee flags in commemoration of martyred students of the twenty-third. Student Jorge Navarro intensifies urban clandestine work of Sandinist Front, initiates circulation of clandestine publication *Trinchera*. September: red and black flag of Sandinist Front appears in Leon. Strikes of stevedores, construction workers, carpenters, business employees, etc. Arrests connected with arms traffic. Somoza denounces "communist conspiracy directed from Cuba." October: peasant group with rudimentary arms confronts army elements on El

Bijao mountain. November: installation of first congress of secondary education, organized by Student Club of Ramirez Goyena Institute. Various government and reactionary organizations demand intervention of OEA (Organization of American States) in Nicaragua to pacify "terrorism."

1963 February: revolutionary student congress. Persecution of young revolutionaries. March: military man Juan Angel Lopez, later guilty of Posoltega crimes, threatens workers. March: Sandinist Front squad occupies radio station by force and makes statement against meeting held by Kennedy in Costa Rica with Central American puppets. May 30: Sandinist Front "expropriation" at a bank. Army mobilizes forces that include small aircraft. Truck drivers, stevedores, construction workers unions are active. Government dissolves many unions. July-October: intensified activity of Sandinist Front in mountains of Rio Coco and Rio Bocay. Assassinations in mountains of guerrilla fighters Jorge Navaro, Modesto Duarte and several others. October: national student strike condemning ferocious repression of regime against guerrilla elements. December: young Nicaraguan rebels arrested and tortured in Guatemala by local cops and Cuban *gusanos* from the counter-revolutionary Alfa-66. Selim Schible and Edmundo Perez among them. Handed over to Nicaraguan GN.

1964 CONDECA, coordinating organization of Central American armies, begins representing Yankee State Department at regional level. January: acts of solidarity with people of Panama, immediately after North American repression. Panamanian flag raised on a Matagalpa hill. February: massive student actions in solidarity with Sandinist prisoner survivors. Regime accuses students of attempting massive action to rescue Sandinist prisoners from place where they were held. In order to recover from attacks by Somoza terror, Sandinist Front intensifies its work with massive sectors of peasants. Alesio Gutierrez turns up to dissolve a demonstration favouring literacy campaign. May 1: a peasant representative, participating in massive celebration of the date in the city of Matagalpa, exclaims: "Long live the Sandinist Front!" June: first legal strike in the country's union history. Supreme court of labour authorizes Singer strike. Bluefields union, Atlantic coast, protests for new customs laws. "We're Nicaraguans and they examine us when we travel to Managua . . ." July: massive student actions denouncing anti-Sandinist repression. December: imprisoned rebels Selim Schible and Edmundo

Perez, among others, accused of attempts to take over barracks in
Belen and Potosi.

1965 January: Carlos Fonseca deported to Guatemala. February:
much painting and displaying of Sandinist slogans in the capital: many
young people arrested. April: bombs explode on Somoza property in
Esteli. Popular and student actions denouncing imperialist intervention in Dominican Republic. July: arrests in Esteli of youths accused of
distributing Sandinist propaganda. September: patriotic march of
more than 40 kilometers to San Jacinto, headed by Julio Buitrago and
Francisco Moreno. November: peasants tortured in Bocaycito for
reclaiming land.

1966 Delegate of FSLN attends fourth OCLAE conference in
Havana. Death of Marvin Guerrero, Sandinist militant brutallly
tortured when arrested by gang in Chinendaga. January: worker
Carlos Reina attends first Tri-continental Congress in Havana, as
delegate of Sandinist Front. February: people's solidarity with
Vietnam. Brutal seizure of students in "Maestro Gabriel" Institute.
April: Sandinist Front intesifies activities. May: Enrique Lorente,
Selim Schible and other youths seized and accused of preparing
attempts against tyranny. May 1: student Casimiro Sotelo forms part
of National Committee to celebrate May First, months before, Sotelo
and Julio Buitrago visited mining centers and formulated denunciation of cruel exploitation by foreign monopolies. July-October: Oscar
Turcios and other members of the Sandinist Front do a stint with the
Guatemala guerillas. July: seizure of students of Journalism School
and hunger strike protesting candidacy of Somoza. Revolutionary
students publish *The Student*. Burning of Somocists' vehicles to
protest proclamation of presidential candidacy of Anastasio Somoza
Debayle. July 23: national student day celebrated for first time on
campus of Catholic University, resulting in expulsion of Casimiro
Sotelo. In extensive actions students carry placards with pictures of
martyrs and the text: SOMOZA GAVE THE ORDER. September:
Sandinist front reinforces rural work directed toward recruiting
guerrillas. October: group of students appear in national stadium
before the masses displaying big placard with slogan: NO MORE
SOMOZA. Bloody repression. November: circulation of Sandinist
Front document calling for armed struggle by the people and
proclaiming SANDINO YES, SOMOZA NO, and INSURRECTION
YES, ELECTORAL FARCE NO. Opposition elements publicly
assassinated in various parts of the country.

1967   January: "expropriation" at branch of San Sebastian bank.
January 22: bloody maneuver by bourgeois opposition sector,
according to offical figures, 201 peasants killed in Managua.
February: letter of lyceum member Francisco Moreno is circulated
explaining his joining the activity of Sandinist Front. April: execution
in Esteli of Somocist Concepcion Rayo, ex-member of so-called
"Fateful Squad" of Chinandega. May: bombs in Somocist
warehouses. "Expropriations" in Lacmiel and of an armored car of a
Nicaraguan bank. Extensive persecutions against persons accused of
cooperating with Sandinist Front. Massive student anti-Somocist
actions. June: "expropriation" at a branch of Bank of London on
Kennedy Boulevard. July: denunciation of torture with electric shock.
Delegation of Sandinist Front, presided over by student Casimiro
Sotelo, attends OLAS conference. Lockout of lyceum members in
Matagalpa. Student congress "Martyrs of Liberation." Red and black
flags appear in Leon. Armed military elements attack striking
economics students. Lockout of lyceum members in Esteli. August:
Selim Schible falls in action in Managua. After several months of
organizing guerrilla groups in mountains, Silvio Mayorga, Danilo
Rosales and other members of Sandinist Front killed at hands of
Somocist forces. Anastasio Somoza Debayle confesses that his forces
suffered "some damage." Bloody repression against peasants.
September: government newspaper *Novedades* prints news that
Anastasio Somoza Debayle, in Jinotega ". . . ANNOUNCES
EXTERMINATION OF GUERRILLAS." October: 16-year-old Sandin-
ist militant, Rene Carrion, is accused of terrorism and assassinated.
Execution of agent of repression Gonzalo Lecayo. Newspaper *La
Prensa* publishes document signed by Chamber of Industry,
Nicaraguan Institute of Development, Association of Banking
Institutions, and Cooperative of Nicaraguan Cotton Dealers, S.A., all
institutions of the high bourgeoisie, calling for "unified action"
against insurrectional movement. November: *Novedades* prints:
SOMOZA ORDERS EXTERMINATION OF URBAN GUERRILLAS.
Casimiro Sotelo and three other clandestine militants of Sandinist
Front captured in middle of the city, in broad daylight, and
assassinated. Boy of twelve, arrested near Managua, suspected of
cooperating with Sandinists, tortured at hand of GN.

1968   February: clandestine work continues. Document of Sandinist
Front circulates clandestinely on February 21. April: student and
ex-army officer David Tejada, member of Sandinist Front, tortured

atrociously and assassinated; his body thrown into crater of Santiago volcano. Massive actions of students denouncing repression. June: vehicles of Somocists burned in condemnation of President Johnson's passing through Nicaragua. September: "expropriation" in a banking agency of Buenos Aires, Managua. One member of the GN killed. October: extensive student actions commemorating fall of Che. December: capture of some clandestine Sandinist militants.

1969   January-August: repression in Costa Rica against members of Sandinist Front on clandestine mission. February-March: guerrilla actions in Yaosca including clashes with GN and execution of informers. Document about Sandinist Front circulated in Managua. June: "expropriation" in banking agency of Central America quarter. Sandinist leader Oscar Turcios arrested and deported to Spain by Costa Rican authorities. Sandinist militant wounded in frontier clash with GN and political police. Enemy suffers more than three casualties. Sandinist leader Julio Buitrago clandestinely directs an apprenticeship in molotov cocktails and other incendiary bombs for more than 200 young people. July: assassination of several peasants from Las Bayas mountain region. Repression increases. Hundreds of Somoza's troops, backed by tanks and aircraft, attack Sandinist urban refugees in Las Delicias and Santo Domingo. Leader Julio Buitrago at one point and three fighters at another, put up resistance for several hours before dying. Ferocious repression gives rise to gigantic anti-Somocist mobilization by students with participation of women. August: military order given to radio stations not to mention name of tortured prisoner Doris Tijerino. November: Revolutionary Student Front with openly Sandinist slogans achieves success for CUUN in university elections. On November 4 two guerrilla actions on day commemorating anniversary of death of Casimiro Sotelo and other comrades. December: action in Alajuela, Costa Rica, with object of rescuing imprisoned comrade. Armed clash between Sandinists and GN in La Virgen, with favourable outcome for rebels.

1970   Sandinist Jacinto Baca falls in combat in Rota. January: poet Leonel Rugama and two other militants of the Sandinist Front, confronting enormous forces, die in urban refuge; protesting those events at the time, the priest Francisco Mejia is arrested and beaten. 90 kilometer march, Leon-Managua, of students in favour of political prisoners and other revolutionary demands. February-March: guerrilla actions in Zinica mountain region. Failure of Somocist attempts to hide their casualties. Among government's losses: one helicopter. Armed occupation of radio station and broadcasting of revolutionary message on February 21. April: Officer Fernando Cadeno assassinated by Somocist army troops themselves in reprisal for certain honest viewpoints of his. Facing attack of enormous Somocist forces at an urban location in Leon, workers Enrique Lorente and Luisa Amanda Espinoza, both Sandinists, are killed on April 3. GN officer Ernesto Abaunza executed. Assassinations of peasants by GN elements in mountains of Atlantic coast. May-June: hunger strike of mothers and students on behalf of political prisoners; prisoners also strike. In May, assassination of three guerrilla fighters captured on highway in Tuma region. "Expropriation" in Boer Bank branch. July: GN forces use repressive methods in Esteli. Posters referring to Sandinist Front appear on Rivas streets. August: Arbolito clash: armed encounter between Sandinists and GN with favourable outcome for the revolutionaries. Somocist armed aggression against Catholic University campus. September: death of Patricio Arguello, member of Sandinist Front, in guerrilla action supporting Palestinian people. Massive national protest in all cities of country against Somocist repression of Sandinist militants. Denunciation of assassinations of peasants in Zinica highlands. October: several members of Sandinist Front rescued from Costa Rican prison by means of guerrilla action. General strike of educational workers rasing union demands, backed by students. Leon-Managua march of students in solidarity with striking teachers. On October 21 people rejoice, singing in streets, fireworks, etc., on occasion of the rescue of Nicaraguan prisoners in Costa Rica. November: protest by students of architecture against Central American Congress of Architecture.

1971 January: protest actions by students of Catholic University. Actions of Leon students because of transportation price increase. February: assassination of peasant Maximo Martinez and Pedro Guerrero in El Chile after their participation in peaceful union activities. April: assassination of Efrain Gonzalez and Rommel Lopez after their participation in peaceful union protests. Repressive Honduran elements on the border persecute Nicaraguans accused of revolutionary activity. Hunger strike of prisoners backed by their mothers and other family members, protesting brutal treatment received. Massive student actions on behalf of Sandinist prisoners. Peasant group protests repression. Extensive arrests of students and their families in Managua. One North American identified among repressive Somocist elements attacking Managua cathedral. Anasta-

sio Somoza Debayle declares in report to his national "congress" that
his regime has faced "subversive and terrorist activity." May:
military force, including helicopters, used against popular protests in
Matagalpa for recent assassinations. Assassination of peasants in
concentration camp of Cua district. Group of peasants moves to capital
to go on hunger strike protesting repression suffered. June: peasants
Porfirio and Jose Luis Barrera assassinated in mountains. Peasant
group in new action of anti-repressive protest in Managua. Publication
of long list of peasants who had "disappeared." July: it is known that
North American officer Kenneth E. Murphy, with past experience in
Korea, Vietnam, and the Canal Zone, advises the armed forces of the
Somoza regime. Air and ground military deployment in mountains of
Matagalpa and Jinotega. August: family members denounce risk of
assassination to which Sandinist prisoners are exposed. November:
atrocious murder of young Sandinist Denis Enrique Romero, arrested
in Esteli.

1972   January: prisoner hunger strike, backed by mothers and other
relatives, against brutal treatment suffered. April: intervention of the
Somoza regime's military in crushing of military uprising against
unpopular regime in El Salvador. May: students' and people's
protests against prices of gasoline and milk. June: assassination of
two peasants in El Crucero, near Managua. Mother of victim cries:
"Bury me beside them!" Military maneuver in Nicaragua known as
"Eagle 3," with participation of elements of Central American and
North American armies. July: elements of rural authorities accused of
collaboration with guerrilla struggle. One person imprisoned for
merely possessing photo of Sandino. September: assassination of
peasants in Tepochapa, department of Managua. October: arrests in
Bluefields and Puerto Cabezas, Atlantic coast. November: GN
elements set fire to peasant huts in Pantasma, Jinotega. Massive acts
in Managua claiming freedom for prisoners. Labourer working in
mining center of Bonanza, Atlantic coast, atrociously murdered by
elements of GN: " . . . they tortured him, gouged out his eyes, sewed
his lips together with wire, cut out his tongue . . ." December: hunger
strike by Sandinist prisoners, extensive actions by students
demanding freedom for prisoners. Earthquake in Managua on
December 23: urban chaos of regime has catastrophic consequences;
administrative vandalism shown at its worst.

1973   April-August: system forced labour imposed for rubble
removal; construction workers backed by students engage in strikes

putting forward union demands; health workers and other sectors aid these actions. May: elements of GN set fire to peasant huts in department of Leon. June: Sandinist fighter Artega Nunez assassinated in Leon. Letter circulated, signed by mothers of Sandinist prisoners, claiming freedom for their sons. Among prisoners are young people recruited since 1967. Years of prison suffered by young Sandinists add up to more time than accumulated by political prisoners throughout the previous century in Nicaragua. July: massive student actions backing workers. Workers on banana plantations, controlled by Standard Fruit Company in Chinandega, complain of unfair working conditions. August: several GN deaths in spontaneous actions of Managua workers. September: on September 6 Anastasio Somoza Debayle, attending Tenth Conference of American Armies in Caracas, states that his regime has confronted 23 armed revolutionary raids. GN forces with helicopters attack guerrilla fighters of Sandinist Front in Nandaime zone. Somocist force suffers minimum of casualties, two Sandinist women escape, guns in hand, and Oscar Turcios and Ricardo Morales, both members of Sandinist Front leadership, along with Jonathan Gonzalez and Juan Jose Quezada, are killed. At least two Sandinists assassinated while prisoners. Over 1000 peasants take land in Chinandega. Twenty-three Subtiavan native leaders persecuted by Guard after retaking land. November: strike of Licorera Nacional broken up by GN. December: campaign to free comrade Francisco Ramirez Urbina and Salvadoran professor Efrain Nortlewalton. Twenty-five leaders arrested and tortured.

1974   Armed peasant group kidnaps Somocist landowner. GN squads attack hundreds of peasant families. February: Manuel Aviles assassinated in Rivas. April: comrade Ramon Gonzalez assassinated. North American AIFLD (reactionary unionism) has been working among Nicaraguan unions since 1963. By 1974 it announces having almost 9000 students trained to infiltrate Nicaraguan unions and claims that CIA controls CUS. Peasant population in west regains lands appropriated by GN officers in Palo Alto and Palo Grande. Much repression. Jailing of 48 entire families, children and old people included. Peasants Amada Pineda, Maria Castil and others raped and murdered. May: other peasant men, women and children arrested. Concentration camps holding very young children. Alfredo Medina assassinated, Andres Lopez and others tortured. In New Guinea, a peasant colony in the west, where peasants despoiled of their lands elsewhere are taken; Teresa de Leon Perez is repressed and imprisoned. September: new repression against Subtiavan leaders in

Leon. Student leaders, among them CUN president, who had travelled to Venezuela and Panama, where they had denounced conditions in Nicaragua, arrested. December: on December 27 comando "Juan Jose Quezada" of Sandinist Front enters home of Jose Maria Castillo, Nicaraguan consul in United States, ex-president of National Bank and flatfoot of Somoza regime. Castillo gave party in honour of North American ambassador. Commando kidnaps great number of hostages, all agents of dictatorship or its allies, demands freedom for all political prisoners, $1 million, salary increases for common guards and other exploited sectors, and publication by press and radio of two communiques explaining to the people the terms of the action and denouncing conditions of exploitation and repression suffered by country. Action completely successful for Sandinists.